Project Management Institute

PRACTICE STANDARD FOR SCHEDULING

Second Edition

Library of Congress Cataloging-in-Publication Data

Practice standard for scheduling / Project Management Institute. -- 2nd ed.
    p. cm.
  Includes bibliographical references and index.
  ISBN 978-1-935589-24-2 (pbk. : alk. paper) 1. Project management--Standards. I. Project Management Institute.
  HD69.P75P653 2011
  658.4'04—dc23

                                                                                              2011020603

Published by:
  Project Management Institute, Inc.
  14 Campus Boulevard
  Newtown Square, Pennsylvania 19073-3299 USA.
  Phone: +610-356-4600
  Fax: +610-356-4647
  E-mail: customercare@pmi.org
  Internet: www.PMI.org

PMI Publications welcomes corrections and comments on its books. Please feel free to send comments on typographical, formatting, or other errors. Simply make a copy of the relevant page of the book, mark the error, and send it to: Book Editor, PMI Publications, 14 Campus Boulevard, Newtown Square, PA 19073-3299 USA.

To inquire about discounts for resale or educational purposes, please contact the PMI Book Service Center.
  PMI Book Service Center
  P.O. Box 932683, Atlanta, GA 31193-2683 USA
  Phone: 1-866-276-4764 (within the U.S. or Canada) or +1-770-280-4129 (globally)
  Fax: +1-770-280-4113
  E-mail: info@bookorders.pmi.org

10 9 8 7 6 5 4 3 2

NOTICE

The Project Management Institute, Inc. (PMI) standards and guideline publications, of which the document contained herein is one, are developed through a voluntary consensus standards development process. This process brings together volunteers and/or seeks out the views of persons who have an interest in the topic covered by this publication. While PMI administers the process and establishes rules to promote fairness in the development of consensus, it does not write the document and it does not independently test, evaluate, or verify the accuracy or completeness of any information or the soundness of any judgments contained in its standards and guideline publications.

PMI disclaims liability for any personal injury, property or other damages of any nature whatsoever, whether special, indirect, consequential or compensatory, directly or indirectly resulting from the publication, use of application, or reliance on this document. PMI disclaims and makes no guaranty or warranty, expressed or implied, as to the accuracy or completeness of any information published herein, and disclaims and makes no warranty that the information in this document will fulfill any of your particular purposes or needs. PMI does not undertake to guarantee the performance of any individual manufacturer or seller's products or services by virtue of this standard or guide.

In publishing and making this document available, PMI is not undertaking to render professional or other services for or on behalf of any person or entity, nor is PMI undertaking to perform any duty owed by any person or entity to someone else. Anyone using this document should rely on his or her own independent judgment or, as appropriate, seek the advice of a competent professional in determining the exercise of reasonable care in any given circumstances. Information and other standards on the topic covered by this publication may be available from other sources, which the user may wish to consult for additional views or information not covered by this publication.

PMI has no power, nor does it undertake to police or enforce compliance with the contents of this document. PMI does not certify, test, or inspect products, designs, or installations for safety or health purposes. Any certification or other statement of compliance with any health or safety-related information in this document shall not be attributable to PMI and is solely the responsibility of the certifier or maker of the statement.

TABLE OF CONTENTS

LIST OF TABLES AND FIGURES

PREFACE

The *Practice Standard for Scheduling*—Second Edition has been developed as a complement to *A Guide to the Project Management Body of Knowledge* (*PMBOK® Guide*—Fourth Edition) in the Knowledge Area of Project Time Management. This second edition of the practice standard builds upon the foundation established by the first edition describing the methods related to scheduling that are generally recognized as good practice for *most projects most of the time*. Good practice means that there is general agreement that the correct application of these skills, tools, and techniques can enhance the chances of success over a wide range of different projects. Good practice does not mean that the knowledge described should always be applied uniformly on all projects; *the project management team is responsible for determining what is appropriate for any given project*.

The project management community has strongly voiced the need for a standard to promote the development of sound schedules. In addition, the community asked for the capability to assess the adequacy of their schedules.

This practice standard is designed to provide project management practitioners, who are familiar with the *PMBOK® Guide*—Fourth Edition, with a summary of the benefits and advantages of a well-developed and maintained schedule model. This practice standard describes the hallmarks of a sound and effective project scheduling methodology, as well as providing quantifiable means for assessing the application of the provisions of this standard to a schedule model.

One of the most significant developments in the creation of the first edition of the *Practice Standard for Scheduling* centered upon the clarification of the term *schedule*. It became apparent through the discussion process and the community feedback that there was significant support for the clarification of this terminology. The *Practice Standard for Scheduling*—Second Edition clarified this distinction between the project schedule and schedule model.

Schedule development flows from the selection of an appropriate *scheduling method* followed by selection and use of a *scheduling tool*. Next, project-specific data is entered into the *scheduling tool* to produce the *schedule model*. From there, instances of the *schedule model* are saved for use as what-if platforms, targets, and for formal approval as a baseline. From these instances, various *presentations* are produced for a wide range of uses. With these discrete terms, project management practitioners have the ability to trace the processes from the *PMBOK® Guide*—Fourth Edition to the finished product and answer, in a specific and unambiguous way, the question of what is being requested when you are asked for a schedule.

The *Practice Standard for Scheduling*—Second Edition focused on adding more clarity to the issues and concepts of the previous edition:

- Chapter 2 was reorganized to align more closely with the *PMBOK® Guide*—Fourth Edition with specific emphasis on schedule model management and providing additional clarity on the various schedule methods and techniques.

- Chapter 3 was reorganized to emphasize good practices in the areas of model management, model creation, maintenance, analysis, and communication and reporting.

- Chapter 4 remains focused on the various components of a schedule model. The update introduces the concept of four *required* component groups in addition to two *optional* components groups. This refinement was developed to address areas of concern raised from the 2007 edition, broadening the scope of coverage to earned value, risk, and the application of resources.

- Chapter 5 was rewritten to continue to allow for the assessment of a schedule model within the more complex guidelines of multiple required and optional components. It also addressed a concern expressed from the previous edition concerning the assessment process.

This practice standard is consistent with the *PMBOK® Guide*—Fourth Edition. It also includes information from accepted project management practices from many industries. The Project Management Institute standards program will continue to periodically update this standard as part of the overall planned evolution of PMI standards documents. Comments from project management practitioners are both requested and welcome.

CHAPTER 1

INTRODUCTION

This chapter is designed to provide an overview of the content of this practice standard. This chapter is divided into the following sections:

1.1 Project Scheduling

1.2 Why Scheduling

1.3 Overview

1.4 Purpose

1.5 Applicability

Each section provides additional information on the content and terminology used in this practice standard.

1.1 Project Scheduling

Project scheduling is the application of skills, techniques, and intuition acquired through knowledge and experience to develop effective schedule models. The schedule model integrates and logically organizes various project components, such as activities, resources, and logical relationships, to enhance the likelihood of successful project completion within the baseline duration.

The terms schedule model, schedule model instance, and presentations are defined in the glossary of the standard. These terms are described below:

Schedule model is a dynamic representation of the plan for executing the project activities developed by the project stakeholders, applying a selected scheduling method to a scheduling tool using project-specific data. The schedule model can be processed by a scheduling tool to produce various schedule model instances.

Schedule model instance is a copy of the schedule model, that has been processed by a schedule tool and has reacted to inputs and adjustments made to the project specific data within the scheduling tool (completed update cycle), that is saved for record and reference, such as data date version, target schedule models, and the baseline schedule model. The instances produce various schedule presentations such as critical paths, resource profiles, activity assignments, record of accomplishments, etc., and can provide time-based forecasts throughout the project's life cycle. When used together, the instances support analysis, such as variance analysis.

Presentation is an output from schedule model instances, used to communicate project-specific data for reporting, analysis, and decision making.

1.2 Why Scheduling?

Projects are generally complex endeavors; however, a detailed schedule model may result in decomposing projects into manageable phases or groupings. Project performance is then reported and monitored when progress against these activities and milestones is recorded. As progress is recorded on a project, the remaining effort requires reassessment. The execution of a project often does not proceed exactly as it was initially planned and baselined. In a typical project environment, because of inadequate planning or significant project changes, it becomes necessary to refine the schedule model. This iterative evolution is required to predict, recognize, and address those evolving factors and issues that will potentially affect project performance. The key to project success is to apply knowledge and experience to create a project management plan and then commit to execute the project according to the plan. Scheduling is one of the basic requirements of project management planning and analysis.

Scheduling provides a detailed plan that represents how and when the project will deliver the products, services, and results defined in the project scope and may serve as a tool for communication, managing stakeholder expectations, and as a basis for performance reporting. The dynamic nature of a project's execution is best served by a tool that allows for modeling of the project, the project internal and external dependencies, and analysis due to the impact of progress and unforeseen developments.

The schedule model supports the project by allowing for:

- Time phasing of required activities
- Mobilization of resources in a most efficient manner
- Coordination of events within the project and between other projects
- Early detection of risks or problems
- Implementation of actions to achieve the project objectives as planned
- Allowing for "what-if" analysis
- Resource planning
- Forecasting of estimate at complete

1.3 Overview

This *Practice Standard for Scheduling* describes schedule model components (see Chapter 4) and generally recognized good practices for scheduling processes. "Generally recognized" means that the knowledge and practices described are applicable to most projects most of the time; there is consensus about their value and usefulness. "Good practice" means that there is general agreement that the application of these skills, tools, and techniques can enhance the probability of success over a wide range of projects. Good practice does not mean the knowledge described should always be applied uniformly to all projects; the project team is responsible for determining what is appropriate for any given project. The proper use of the components and their practices results in a schedule model usable for planning, executing, monitoring, closing, and the delivery of the project scope to stakeholders. The Create Schedule process begins with selecting a scheduling method and scheduling tool that support the desired scheduling method, followed by incorporating project-specific data within that scheduling tool, thus creating a unique schedule model." The result is a schedule model instance used to generate various presentations and reports. See Figure 1-1 to better understand the interrelationships of the schedule model creation concepts and terminology. This process results in a schedule model for project execution, monitoring, and control that will respond predictably to progress and changes. The schedule model is regularly updated to reflect progress and changes such as scope, durations, milestones, allocated resources, productivity rates, work methodology, or scheduling logic. This *Practice Standard for Scheduling* also provides an assessment process that can be used to determine how well the schedule model conforms to this standard. A conformance index (see Chapter 5 of this practice standard) is developed by determining which components are used and how they are used within the schedule model. To obtain an acceptable conformance assessment, a schedule model, at a minimum, should contain all of the required components as described in Chapter 4 and Appendix D. The selection of an appropriate scheduling software tool provides access to the required components necessary to develop the schedule model. The use of this practice standard, along with experience, skill, and organizational maturity, will guide the proper application of the components.

The inclusion of a component in this practice standard does not necessarily bear any relation to the issues of project size or complexity. This practice standard assumes that all schedule models need to have the required components, basic behaviors, and good practices; project size and complexity only result in changes in scale and repetition of the required components. *A Guide to the Project Management Body of Knowledge (PMBOK® Guide)*—Fourth Edition provides processes to address the factors regarding project size and complexity. In addition, the definition of "generally recognized" also assumes that there are no significant differences for the use of the required components as to the scheduling practices within various industries. As practices evolve and develop within the project management community after the publication of this practice standard, the definition of "generally recognized" will also evolve. More components may be added to the core set, and good practices should become less subjective.

1.4 Purpose

The purpose of this *Practice Standard for Scheduling* is to provide guidelines for the effective use of time management for a project by providing knowledge on the creation of schedule models. This practice standard expands on the information contained in Chapter 6 (Project Time Management section) of the *PMBOK® Guide*—Fourth Edition. Further, to properly address the needs voiced by the project management community, it is essential to provide a means to assess the degree of conformance with this practice standard. In doing so, this practice standard establishes a core set of required components to be utilized in order to establish a schedule model that meets a minimum acceptable degree of conformance to this practice standard and a method to access a schedule model for conformance to this standard. The set of components required for each schedule model should be described in the project's schedule model management plan (see Section 3.1).

The ultimate goal of this practice standard is to create schedule models that are of increasing value to the projects they represent.

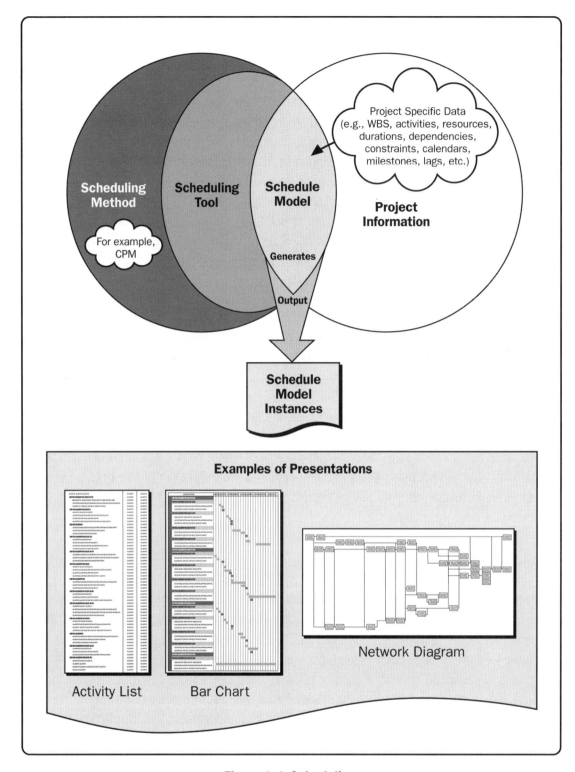

Figure 1-1. Scheduling

It is not the purpose of this practice standard to provide a comprehensive guide on how to develop a schedule model. For comprehensive instruction on developing a schedule model, refer to courses and text books on the subject.

1.5 Applicability

This practice standard targets project management practitioners who are knowledgeable in the fundamentals of project scheduling. For the purposes of this practice standard, these practitioners will be known as schedulers.

It is the premise of this practice standard that: the reader has a basic working knowledge of the Project Management Process Groups and Knowledge Areas as defined in the *PMBOK® Guide*—Fourth Edition, the project has a work breakdown structure (WBS) that conforms to the processes defined in the *Practice Standard for Work Breakdown Structures*—Second Edition, and that the appropriate planning has occurred. As schedule development progresses, related practice standards such as the *Practice Standard for Earned Value Management*—Second Edition may be applied.

This practice standard is applicable to individual projects only—not programs or portfolios. However, because programs and portfolios are collections of individual projects, any individual schedule model within those structures should make use of, and be evaluated according to this practice standard.

Furthermore, an organization that embraces the principles and good practices outlined in this standard and applies them globally across the organization ensures that all of the schedule models developed in support of the organization's projects are done in a consistent manner throughout the organization.

CHAPTER 2

THE SCHEDULE MODEL PRINCIPLES AND CONCEPTS

This chapter is designed to provide guidance and information on the principles and concepts associated with the schedule model creation and use. This chapter is divided into the following sections:

2.1 Overview

2.2 Scheduling Methods

2.3 Scheduling Techniques

2.4 The Scheduling Tool

2.5 The Schedule Model

2.6 The Schedule Model Instances and Presentations

Each section provides additional requirements, terminology, and associated functionality with these topics. These sections link the processes described in this chapter to the good practices described in Chapter 3 and the scheduling components defined in Chapter 4.

2.1 Overview

The schedule model principles and concepts are depicted in Figure 2-1. The schedule model management plan identifies the scheduling method and the scheduling tool utilized to create the schedule model. The Create Schedule process incorporates all of the defined processes associated with the project scheduling effort (Initiating, Planning, Executing, Monitoring and Controlling, and Closing). Within this modeling process, all of the required project activities and milestones are defined and sequenced to achieve the project objectives. The Create Schedule process includes the Define Activities, Sequence Activities, Estimate Activity Resources, Estimate Activity Durations, and Develop Schedule processes (see the *PMBOK® Guide*—Fourth Edition). The schedule model can generate schedule model instances which produce presentations (See Figure 2-1). The schedule model instances can include, the approved baseline, selected targets, and what-if schedule models. The Create Schedule process results in an approved schedule model used by the processes in the Executing and Monitoring and Controlling Process Groups (see the *PMBOK® Guide*—Fourth Edition), which reacts predictably and logically to project progress and changes. Once created and approved (baseline established) the schedule model is updated, as necessitated by project performance and in support of the project's regular reporting intervals, to reflect progress and changes.

During project planning, a process to create a schedule model that meets the needs of the project and its stakeholders begins.

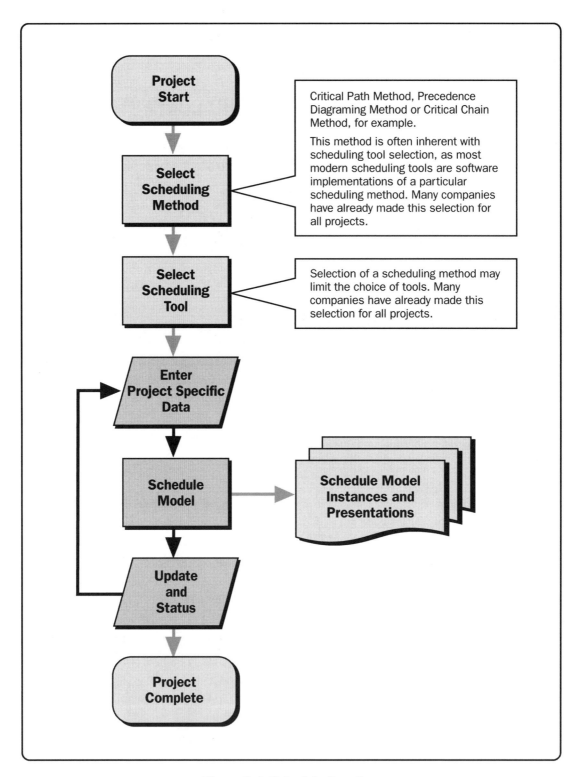

Figure 2-1. Schedule Creation

Many of the terms and concepts discussed in this overview are explained in greater detail in Chapter 3 of this practice standard. Defined activities, based on the project WBS, need to be identified and described uniquely, starting with a verb, include at least one unique specific object, and clarifying adjectives when necessary. Activities are sequenced with appropriate logical relationships. The quantity, skill level, and capabilities of the resources required to complete each activity should be considered, in addition to consulting the activity performers when determining the duration of each activity. Constraints, including lead/lag time factors, should not be used in the schedule model to replace schedule logic. The schedule model creation provides a baseline to permit comparison of progress against the approved plan. An overview of the Create Schedule process is illustrated in the flow diagram and process component mapping table shown in Figures 2-2(a) and 2-2(b).

2.2 Scheduling Methods

The scheduling method provides the framework for schedule model creation. The most common scheduling method, supported by all the major scheduling tools, is the precedence diagram method (PDM). With this common and pervasive usage, it is often referred to as the critical path method (CPM). Another popular method is critical chain which is based on CPM. Within these methods, there are various techniques such as rolling wave, PERT, Monte Carlo, integrated master scheduling, and agile. The first step in the Create Schedule process is the selection of an appropriate method and technique. Some organizations standardize on a specific software tool. In this case, the scheduling method decision has already been made, as it is inherent in the tool, and does not need to be made again. Since it is the most commonly used method, this practice standard focuses on CPM.

2.2.1   Critical Path Method

The critical path method (CPM) determines the minimum total project duration and the earliest possible finish date of the project as well as the amount of scheduling flexibility (total float) in the schedule model. To apply CPM, a schedule model is developed, which is comprised of project activities. Early start and finish dates are calculated for each activity by means of a forward pass, from a specific project date. Late start and finish dates are determined for each activity by means of a backward pass, starting from the project early finish date determined during the forward pass calculation or from a specific project finish date (constraint).

A basic principle of CPM is that each activity will be finished before its successor can begin. Without various enhancements, the pure CPM network allows only zero or positive total float. Pure CPM does not accommodate many of the commonplace features of today's scheduling applications; including resource, project and activity calendars, constraints, varying definitions of criticality, resources, elapsed durations, lags, external dependencies, activity priorities, and the assigning of actual start and finish dates to activities.

In common usage, the term CPM refers to the prevalent method used in modern scheduling tools. In these tools, the actual method is usually the precedence diagram method (PDM) and this practice standard follows that common usage convention.

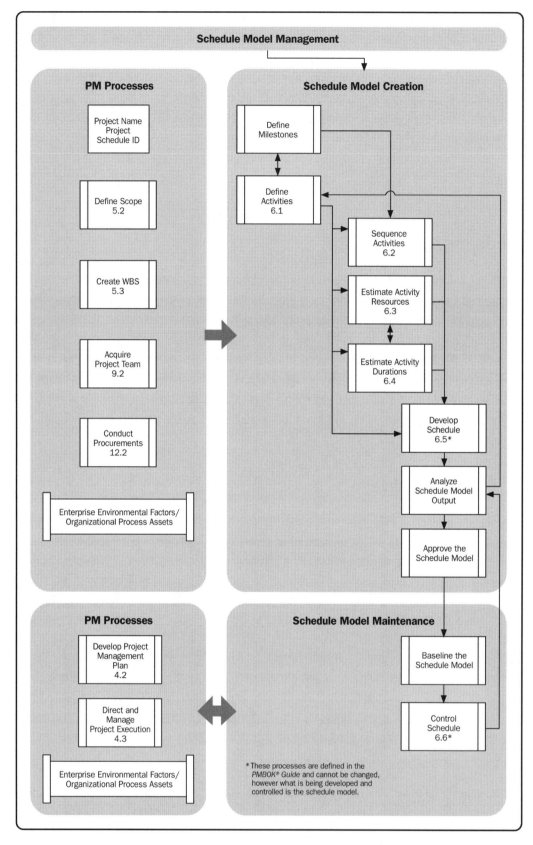

Figure 2-2(a). Flow Diagram for the Schedule Model

Activity	Component	Use	Activity	Component	Use
Schedule Model Management	Control Account Manager (CAM)	O	Develop Schedule (6.5) (cont'd)	Probability Risk Distribution	KRC
	Earned Value Method	O		Project Early Finish Date	R
	Project Calendar	R		Project Early Start Date	R
	Project Cost Category	O		Project Finish Constraint	O
	Project Description	O		Project Late Finish Date	R
	Project Manager	O		Project Late Start Date	R
	Project Name	R		Project Resource Leveled Finish Date	O
	Resource Library/Dictionary	RRC		Project Resource Leveled Start Date	O
	Resource Rates/Prices	O		Project Start Constraint	O
	Schedule Model ID	R		Resource Lag	O
	Unit of Measure	R		Resource Leveling	O
	Custom Field	O		Total Float	R
Define Milestones, Define Activities (6.1)	Activity Calendar	O	Baseline the Schedule Model	Activity Original Duration	R
	Activity Code	O		Baseline Schedule Model	R
	Activity ID	R	Control Schedule (6.6)	Activity Actual Cost	ERC
	Activity Label	R		Activity Actual Duration	R
	Activity Risk Criticality Index	KRC		Activity Actual Finish Date	R
	Milestones	R		Activity Actual Start Date	R
	Risk ID	KRC		Activity Physical % Complete OR Activity Duration % Complete	R
	Summary Activity	O		Activity Remaining Duration	R
	WBS ID	ERC		Activity Resource Actual Quantity	RRC
	Work Package Identifier	ERC		Activity Resource Total Quantity	RRC
Sequence Activities (6.2)	Activity Scope Definition	O		Activity Total Duration	R
	Finish Not Later Than	O		Activity Work Percent Complete	O
	Finish to Finish	O		Change Request Identifier	O
	Finish to Start	R		Control Account ID	ERC
	Start to Start	O		Cost Performance Index (CPI)	O
Estimate Activity Resources (6.3)	Activity Cost Category	O		Cost Variance % (CV%)	O
	Activity Cost Estimate	O		Cost Variance (CV)	O
	Activity Effort/Work	O		Data Date	R
	Driving Resources	O		Earned Value (EV)	ERC
	Resource Assignment	RRC		Earned Value Weight	O
	Resource Availability	RRC		Estimate at Completion (EAC)	ERC
	Resource Calendar	RRC		Estimate to Completion (ETC)	ERC
	Resource Description	RRC		Planned Value	ERC
	Resource ID	RRC		Project Actual Duration	R
	Resource Type	RRC		Project Actual Finish Date	R
Estimate Activity Duration (6.4)	Activity Cumulative Probability Risk Distribution	KRC		Project Actual Start Date	R
	Activity Most Likely Duration	KRC		Project Physical % Complete OR Project Duration % Complete	R
	Activity Optimistic Duration	KRC		Project Remaining Duration	R
	Activity Pessimistic Duration	KRC		Project Resource Actual Quantity	RRC
Develop Schedule (6.5)	Activity Early Finish Date	R		Project Resource Total Quantity	RRC
	Activity Early Start Date	R		Project Schedule Level	O
	Activity Late Finish Date	R		Project Total Duration	R
	Activity Late Start Date	R		Schedule Performance Index (SPI)	O
	Activity Resource Leveled Finish Date	O		Schedule Variance % (SV%)	O
	Activity Resource Leveled Start Date	O		Schedule Variance (SV)	O
	Budget At Completion (BAC)	ERC		Target Schedule Model	O
	Critical Path	R		To Complete Performance Index (TCPI)	O
	Free Float	R		Variance	O
	Lag	O	Schedule Model Maintenance	Presentation	R
				Schedule Model Version	R

Fig 2-2(b). Process Component Mapping Table

Practice Standard for Scheduling — Second Edition
©2011 Project Management Institute, 14 Campus Blvd., Newtown Square, PA 19073-3299 USA

2.2.2　Precedence Diagram Method

The original concept of CPM was a computerized modeling process using the activity-on-arrow style of diagramming. The precedence diagramming method (PDM) was introduced a few years later as a "non-computerized approach to scheduling" offering a cleaner, easier to follow, graphical representation of the network; it depicted the activities involved in a project as boxes or nodes, and introduced enhanced logical relationships (in addition to finish-to-start) and the use of leads and lags. The resulting output is a precedence diagram, also known as project network diagram. The PDM approach to CPM was quickly computerized, and modern scheduling tools place the activities on nodes with arrows linking activities; activity nodes may contain information about duration, cost, resources, and constraints. The addition of multiple project calendars and project-specific constraints further complicate the CPM calculations and the analysis of the network. Today's computerized scheduling applications make it much easier to deal with these factors during the schedule model calculation. The end result is that for most projects, the critical path is no longer a zero float path, as was present in early CPM. The resulting output is a precedence diagram, also known as project network diagrams. The PDM places activities on nodes with arrows linking activities; activity nodes may contain information about duration, cost, resources, and constraints. PDM takes fewer nodes than ADM to describe the same set of project data. Although the addition of multiple calendars and constraints further complicate the forward and backward pass calculations and the network analysis of the PDM network, today's computerized scheduling applications complete the additional calculations without problems. In most projects the critical path is no longer a zero float path, as it was in early CPM.

Precedence diagrams illustrate the relationships between activities left to right (time-phased), allowing project activities to flow from a project start milestone to the project complete milestone. Relationships between time-phased activities are represented by directional arrows. The logical relationships need to be satisfied.

To establish a meaningful critical path, it is necessary to develop a logic-based network of activities with empirically derived durations for execution in a realistic and practical manner. Open ends in a schedule are those activities that lack a predecessor and/or a successor activity, thereby creating a hole or gap in the schedule logic from project start to finish. The only open ends that should be expected are the project start and project finish milestones. The use of constraints, including leads and lags, should be restricted to those conditions that cannot be adequately defined and modeled by the application of activity logic.

In PDM, an activity can be connected from either its start or its finish. This allows a start-to-finish logic presentation with no need to break the work down further. Another characteristic of PDM diagrams is the use of lead and lag components.

An example of a precedence diagram is shown in Figure 2-3.

2.2.3　Critical Chain Method

Resource availability competes with the ability to execute tasks on the planned dates. As such, many software programs allow resources to be leveled (so that they are not over tasked); this may stretch the project duration and scheduled start and finish dates for activities. The resultant schedule model, considering the availability of resources, is often called a resource constrained critical path and it is the starting point for critical

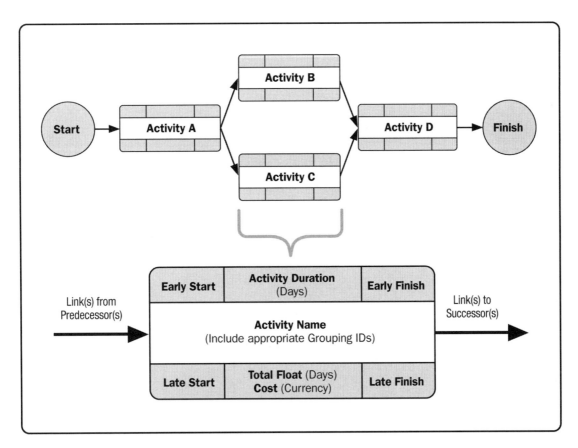

Figure 2-3. Example of CPM/PDM Diagram

chain scheduling. The critical chain method is developed from the CPM approach and considers the effects of resource allocation, resource leveling, and activity duration uncertainty on the CPM-determined critical path. To do so, the critical chain method introduces the concept of buffers and buffer management. Three types of buffers are feeding buffers, resource buffers, and project buffers:

Feeding Buffers. A buffer (in duration) added to the schedule model at the merge of non-critical paths with the project critical path from the CPM.

Resource Buffers. The frequent passing of forecast finish dates to a predecessor activity alerting the resources of the successor activity to be prepared to start work on the forecast finish date of the predecessor activity.

Project Buffers. A duration added to the end of the project between the last project activity and the final delivery date or contracted completion date.

Buffers are statistically determined and aggregated safety margins assigned to individual chains of activities. Buffers are created by assigning aggressive activity realization times to remove any hidden safety margins and aggregating the resulting savings of planned times into buffers. Instead of spreading the safety margins among all activities, the safety margin is concentrated at the end of a chain and used only if risk (whatever it may be, resulting in resource and duration uncertainties) materializes. This effect is similar to managing the total float and free float in the CPM method. An example of a critical chain is shown in Figure 2-4.

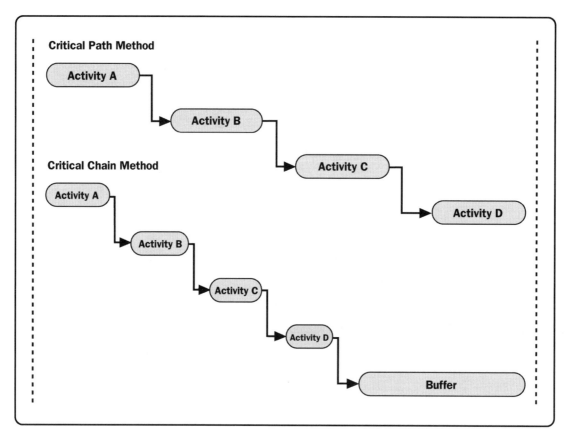

Figure 2-4. Example of Critical Chain

The longest resource-leveled path through the schedule, including buffers, is the critical chain, and it is often different from the critical path in CPM. The defining factors in the critical chain method are buffer activities, resources that are not multi-tasked, resource leveling, and buffer management.

The first step when using the critical chain method for scheduling is to create an aggressive (but not necessarily detailed) resource-leveled project plan. The project end date is defined as the end of the critical chain, including the buffers to account for project risks and slippages. During project execution, if activities consume a longer duration than predicted by the critical chain method, the project buffer is gradually consumed. According to the degree of buffer consumption (also called buffer management), the project team can address necessary corrective actions; from "no need to react" to "planning the response" to "actually executing the planned response to recover project buffer." As long as the total of slippages is less than the buffer, there is limited effect on project scope, duration, and budget.

Critical chain is presented as differing from CPM in four main aspects:

The realization that significant, unexpected risks, which were unforeseen, will materialize during a project and will necessitate proactive actions.

The focus of managerial attention—the critical chain—will remain quite fixed throughout the project.

The resource contention is of such a magnitude in today's lean organizational structures that the duration of projects is dependent on resource availability to no lesser degree than on the logical sequence of activities.

In CPM, a significant margin is contained in all activities, but when exposed and aggregated (instead of being distributed and hidden in individual activities), its risk absorption will be greater by orders of magnitude.

2.3 Scheduling Techniques

Once a scheduling method is established, a group of techniques may be applied to a method. Some of the more common techniques are rolling wave planning, agile scheduling, PERT, and Monte Carlo simulation.

2.3.1   Rolling Wave Planning

Using the rolling wave planning technique, a detailed decomposition of the high-level activities is performed only for those activities in the "near term," for example, the next 90 days. The rolling wave planning technique assumes the project team is very likely to have accurate and detailed information concerning the near-term activities, and less information about activities in the future or later in the project. An important principle for rolling wave planning is to perform the detailed planning at regular intervals. The detailed planning for the next interval needs to be completed well in advance of the start of the next wave's execution.

For periods beyond the detailed planning wave, activities are listed as "planning packages" with much less detail. These planning activities may contain cost and resource information, which becomes fixed in the baseline duration and cost. When detailed planning takes place, it replaces the planning packages with additional details. Figure 2-5 illustrates an example of rolling wave planning.

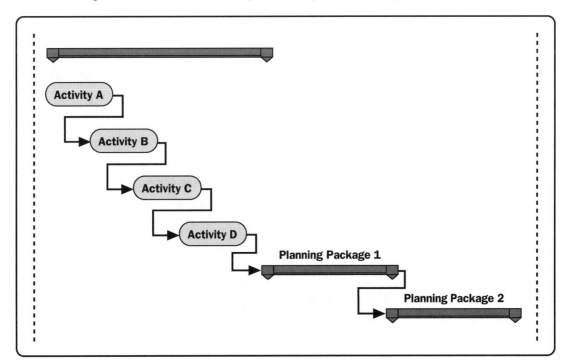

Figure 2-5. Example of Rolling Wave Planning

2.3.2 Agile Technique

Agile project management is similar to rolling wave planning while emphasizing the attainment of usable results quickly and iteratively. The Agile project team utilizes CPM scheduling for each development cycle, called a sprint, which typically lasts two to four weeks. Agile project management focuses on shorter development cycles and tangible results at frequent and incremental intervals; the focus is on realization of interim benefits instead of completing activities. The most important elements of an Agile technique include having multiple iterations of the project phases instead of moving from one phase to another. Another key ingredient of the Agile methods is involvement of the key stakeholders, primarily the customer/end user, at the end of every iteration to approve the interim work products.

2.3.3 Program Evaluation and Review Technique

While similar in principle to CPM and PDM, the program evaluation and review technique (PERT) is focused on activity duration. PERT allows for random activity duration and weights the activity-estimated duration on the range of duration estimates provided by stakeholders. Further development of estimating techniques is provided in the *Practice Standard for Project Estimating*.

Starting with a precedence diagram, PERT allows for activity duration estimates to be determined allowing for the uncertainty contained in the duration estimating process. Three duration estimates are required for each activity:

Optimistic duration (the minimum activity duration under the most favorable conditions)

Most likely duration (the activity duration that will occur most often)

Pessimistic duration (the activity duration under the least favorable conditions)

$$Activity\ Duration_{PERT} = \frac{Optimistic\ Duration + 4\ (Most\ Likely\ Duration) + Pessimistic\ Duration}{6}$$

The durations determined by the previous equation are used in the PERT diagram as activity-estimated durations. Generally durations are established at a specific statistical level of significance (for example, 95% confidence level). The weighting in the equation was a manual approximation of the statistical distribution. With more sophisticated calculations, mostly using computers, an implementation of statistical or multiple simulations PERT (SPERT) is possible, approaching the methods and results of Monte Carlo analysis.

2.3.4 Monte Carlo Simulation

Monte Carlo simulation considers the uncertainty in an activity's duration, cost, resources, and relationships, etc., using the risks from the risk register to drive the uncertainty in activity durations or by estimating those durations directly as optimistic, most likely, and pessimistic estimates for activities. A probability distribution may be assigned to each activity, which considers the confidence level that stakeholders have in the estimates. When there is more confidence in the estimate, a probability distribution with a smaller standard deviation is selected and vice versa.

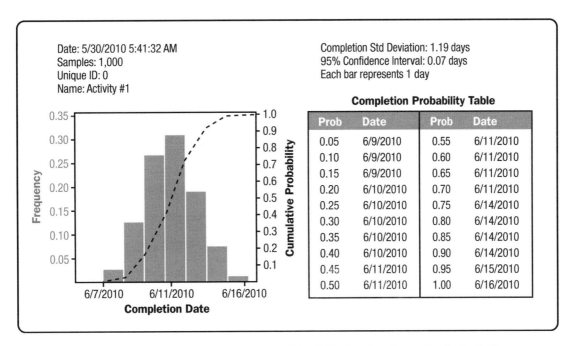

Date: 5/30/2010 5:41:32 AM
Samples: 1,000
Unique ID: 0
Name: Activity #1

Completion Std Deviation: 1.19 days
95% Confidence Interval: 0.07 days
Each bar represents 1 day

Completion Probability Table

Prob	Date	Prob	Date
0.05	6/9/2010	0.55	6/11/2010
0.10	6/9/2010	0.60	6/11/2010
0.15	6/9/2010	0.65	6/11/2010
0.20	6/10/2010	0.70	6/11/2010
0.25	6/10/2010	0.75	6/14/2010
0.30	6/10/2010	0.80	6/14/2010
0.35	6/10/2010	0.85	6/14/2010
0.40	6/10/2010	0.90	6/14/2010
0.45	6/11/2010	0.95	6/15/2010
0.50	6/11/2010	1.00	6/16/2010

Figure 2-6. Example Duration Probability Distribution for a Single Activity

After assigning estimates and probability distributions, the Monte Carlo simulation is run. A simulation is made up of many iterations, each of which represents a possible project result. For each iteration, durations (and resultant costs, etc.) are selected by the Monte Carlo simulation software to be consistent with the probability distributions and activity types specified by the project team. This produces a recorded schedule model instance with attributes for critical path, duration, and cost. This process is then repeated multiple times, resulting in a probability distribution for duration, cost, start dates, and finish dates for each activity selected and ultimately the project. Figure 2-6 shows a sample probability distribution for a single activity.

Further analysis can determine the frequency of specific activities falling on the critical path and the identity of the risks most influential in driving the results at the desired level of certainty. Activities most frequently on the critical path and those that have high-priority risks can be monitored closely to increase the probability that the project will complete on time. Special application software is utilized to complete the Monte Carlo simulation.

2.4 The Scheduling Tool

The scheduling tool is typically a software-specific tool that contains scheduling components and the rules for interrelating these components. Scheduling components are easily visualized by running a scheduling software application and observing the various things in the scheduling tool that are available to build the schedule model.

The scheduling tool is the platform upon which the schedule model is assembled and provides the means to adjust various parameters and components typical in a modeling process. For example, the scheduling tool includes the capability to:

- Select the type of relationship (such as finish-to-start or finish-to-finish) between activities.

- Add lags and leads between activities.

- Apply resources to the activities and use resource information along with resource availability to adjust the scheduling of activities.

- Assign priorities to activities that utilize the same resources over the same period of time.

- Add constraints to activities where logic (e.g., precedence relationships with other activities) alone is not adequate to meet the project requirements, especially when considering external schedule drivers and resource availability.

- Capture a specific schedule model instance as a baseline.

- Perform various what-if-analysis scenarios within the schedule model to obtain different project end dates.

- Analyze the impact potential schedule model changes would have on the project objectives.

- Compare the most recent schedule model instance against a previous schedule model instance or against the approved baseline instance to identify and quantify variances and trends.

2.5 The Schedule Model

The introduction of project-specific data, such as the activities, durations, resources, relationships, and constraints into the scheduling tool creates a schedule model for the given project.

Schedule model analysis compares changes in the schedule model based on updates of progress, cost, and scope with the project team's expectations of the impact of these changes. The project team utilizes the schedule model to predict project finish dates in the form of schedule model instances. The schedule model provides time-based forecasts, reacting to inputs and adjustments made throughout the project's life cycle.

2.6 The Schedule Model Instances and Presentations

The schedule model instance is used to produce presentations for reporting on items, such as critical paths, resource utilization profiles, activity lists, activity assignment lists, records of accomplishment, earned value management system data, time-phased budget, and time-phased costs. The schedule model instances are used to generate various presentations. These outputs of specific project data support the analysis by the project team, including the stakeholders (see Figure 2-7).

A presentation, in its simplest form, is a table of activities with the associated scheduled dates. Presentations are used to communicate to the stakeholders when project activities and events are expected to happen. Resource presentations may also identify the resource, either by a specific person, role or system/tool/etc. that will be required to complete the activities.

The term "schedule" is often used to mean both the schedule model and the output of activities with their associated dates. For clarity and consistency with the *PMBOK® Guide*—Fourth Edition, this practice standard defines the project-specific data within the scheduling tool as a schedule model and the resulting outputs, based on the project specific data, as schedule model instance presentations (see Figures 2-1 and 2-7). Schedule model instance presentations can be represented in many ways, including but not limited to

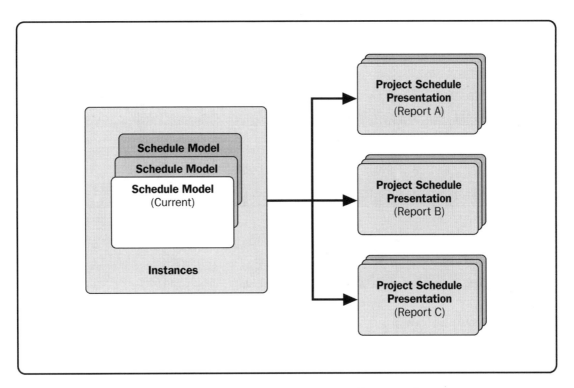

Figure 2-7. Schedule Model Instance Presentations

simple lists, bar charts with dates, network logic diagrams with dates, resource usage patterns, and costs, milestones, master schedules, departmental work lists, team work lists, and deliverable due dates. There are many other possible schedule presentations. Schedule model instance presentations can take the form of an early start schedule, late start schedule, baseline schedule, resource-limited schedule, or target schedule. Other types of schedules are actually derivatives of these five basic schedule types. Such derivatives include master schedules, milestone schedules, and summary schedules. The use of these terms may vary from project to project and organization to organization.

CHAPTER 3

SCHEDULE MODEL GOOD PRACTICES OVERVIEW

This chapter is designed to provide guidance and information on generally accepted good practices associated with the planning, developing, maintaining, communicating, and reporting processes of an effective schedule model. This chapter is divided into the following sections:

3.1 Schedule Model Management

3.2 Schedule Model Creation

3.3 Schedule Model Maintenance

3.4 Schedule Model Analysis

3.5 Communication and Reporting

Each section provides common requirements, terminology, and associated functionality. These sections link the discussion of the schedule processes described in Chapter 2 to the scheduling components defined in Chapter 4. This chapter provides an overview, with examples, of how to create and maintain an effective schedule model.

3.1 Schedule Model Management

Schedule model management encompasses the scheduling-related efforts of the project team as part of the Develop Project Management Plan process in accordance with Section 4.2 of the *PMBOK® Guide*—Fourth Edition. Schedule model management assists in ensuring that all applicable Project Management Process Groups and Knowledge Areas are properly integrated within the overall schedule model. A schedule model requires planning and design in much the same way that every project deliverable is planned and designed. The project team needs to consider a number of factors to create a schedule model that can be a useful tool for the project. This tool will be utilized to monitor performance on the project, communicate information regarding the work, and compare the planned work with the actual progress. These concepts will be developed in support of the Develop Project Management Plan in accordance with the *PMBOK® Guide*.

Schedule model management addresses the following:

- Processes and procedures for schedule model data management such as data formatting, versioning, accessibility, storage, and retrieval of the data.

- Policies related to the methodology that will be used in the schedule model development and maintenance, such as, performance thresholds, content and frequency of presentations and reports, earned value management (EVM) implementation and integration, compatibility with other project plans, risk tracking, and activity granularity. When determining activity granularity, too much detail produces a confusing and overly large schedule model that is difficult and expensive to manage; too little detail means there is insufficient information for the ongoing control of the project.

- Considerations of contractual obligations and potential contract liabilities (claims, mediation, arbitration, litigation, etc.).

- Processes and procedures for planning, updating, and maintaining the schedule model during the project life cycle; determination of an appropriate cycle for gathering the project status and updating the schedule model. The cycle time between updates should be sufficient for the information from the last update to be issued, analyzed, and acted upon by the project team prior to the next update. The update cycle should be in compliance with the contract or organizational process assets.

- Training requirements for the project team members such as a common understanding of scheduling policies, procedures, and software technologies, for example, progress reporting, capturing project risks, and reflecting mitigation activities in the schedule model.

3.1.1   Schedule Data Management Plan

Prior to adding data to the schedule model, the project team should focus on proper schedule model design. The project team needs to define some basic schedule model inputs and expected outputs to ensure that the minimum infrastructure, needed to support stakeholder requirements, is put into place. In addition, the scope, work breakdown structure (WBS), resource definition (when required), and other schedule components should already be defined so that the team does not have to define these elements while developing the schedule model. At a minimum, the project team should consider the following when developing the schedule data management plan:

- Define the list of schedule users, the access rights, and the responsibilities that each will have. For example, some users will provide progress, while others will have greater schedule access and be responsible for administrative functions.

- Determine the frequency (i.e., daily, weekly, or monthly) for backup of the schedule data. Backups are an important part of schedule data configuration management. Required frequencies of backups are often established by stakeholder expectations.

- Determine how previous versions of the schedule will be retrieved, at what intervals, and verify that the procedures for data retrieval are accurate. A common mistake is that backups are performed but there is no retrieval procedure.

- Determine the data retention requirements for the schedule data.

- Identify risks associated with the development of the schedule model related to the schedule data management.

- Determine the data hierarchy requirements for reporting purposes (as defined in the communication plan) and how these requirements will impact the schedule data management process and data model. For example, the types of activities shown to the steering committee are different than those shown to the project manager.

3.1.2 Schedule Model Management Plan

The schedule model management plan is a collection of processes, methods, templates, and tools for accomplishing the project's schedule objectives. Good practice dictates that, all schedule models shall be guided by a methodology that provides a checklist of requirements for the schedule model in order to ensure the quality of the schedule model.

The schedule model management plan enables project team members to perform in a consistent manner. Projects with no plan tend to be inefficient, resulting in higher cost, increased risk, and longer project durations. The schedule model management plan includes the following:

.1 Selection of a Scheduling Method

The project team, with the scheduler as facilitator, should have access to the documentation about the available schedule methods approved by the organization in order to comply with the organizational and project requirements. Based on this information, the scheduler implements the scheduling method as determined by the project team. (For more information about scheduling methods, refer to Section 2.2.)

.2 Selection of a Scheduling Tool

The selection of the scheduling tool will be based on the scheduling method selected and will comply with the organization and project requirements related to the tool.

.3 Schedule Model Creation Plan

The project manager, in conjunction with the project team and key stakeholders, determines the plan for schedule model creation. The key considerations include: rolling wave planning and stakeholder participation in the Develop Schedule process in accordance with the *PMBOK® Guide*—Fourth Edition.

.4 Schedule Model ID

Every schedule model needs to have a unique identification method specific to the project.

.5 Schedule Model Version

Each instance of the schedule model has a unique version identifier. The location of this identification can vary depending on the organizational process assets and tools used to control it. A unique schedule model version identifier is essential to allow the proper archiving of project documents and audit processes. The schedule model management plan will provide the format for this component so that redundant naming does not occur.

.6 Calendars and Work Periods

A default project calendar is defined using work periods. Work periods may also be defined for specific activities or portions of the project including resources. Some of the calendar elements include:

- Define the working days in a week.

- Define the number of shifts to be worked each day.

- Define the number of hours to be worked each shift or day.

- Define any periods of scheduled "overtime" work.

- Define non-working time (e.g., holidays, shutdowns, blackout dates, restricted times, etc.).

These elements play a major role in determining the number and structure of the project calendars required for the schedule. The use of multiple calendars introduces significant complexity to the calculation of float and the critical path. However, while scheduling is simplified by the use of a single calendar, one calendar may be inadequate for managing the project (e.g., an international project team with associated local holidays).

Generally accepted practice is to use a default project calendar that is adequate and reasonable to perform the work, based on the project's normal working times. This project calendar will be used as the default calendar for the project activities. This practice allows the project team to establish and schedule different working periods or calendars, if needed, for certain activities.

.7 Project Update Cycle

The update cycle is the regular interval at which the status of the project is reported. The appropriate frequency for performing updates and reporting status against the schedule is determined. This includes determining at what point in the cycle the update will occur and how often the status will be reported. The update cycle reflects how management intends to utilize the data generated from the schedule model, including the timing of review meetings, management reporting requirements, and payment cycles which often are tied to updates. Select an update cycle providing management with an optimum level of control information without being overly burdensome to the people doing the reporting and analyzing. The optimum update cycle will vary with industry and project intent—from hourly updates for planned outage projects for manufacturing/production facilities to weekly or monthly updates for major construction or software development projects. The chosen update cycle has a direct relationship on the activity durations contained within the schedule.

Experienced practitioners often divide the update cycle into two separate parts: progress reporting and maintenance. This serves to reduce the progress reporting time to a minimum period.

The choice of update cycle is influenced by a number of factors, such as the rate of change in the project, the duration of the project, etc. For relatively stable, long-term, low-risk projects, a monthly or bimonthly status cycle may be appropriate. For volatile, high-risk projects, updates may be required for every shift change or on an hourly basis.

The project team needs to consider which time scale should be used: minutes, hours, days, weeks, or months; the answer depends on the frequency of the control processes and the level of detail needed in the activities. Most of the time, activity time scales will remain consistent throughout the project. However, specific project evolutions can require different time scales effective for that evolution.

.8 Milestone and Activity Coding Structure

Understanding the types of reports, needed from the schedule model to create a presentation (see Figure 2-7) of the schedule model provides guidance on the coding structures to be built into the schedule model.

A coding structure should be developed so that selecting, sorting, and grouping of the schedule data can be easily accomplished. This coding will provide assistance in the development and maintenance of the schedule model, as well as meeting the project reporting requirements. Well-designed coding structures are also helpful in analyzing project performance data by grouping, selection, and sorting to highlight trends and anomalies.

Emphasis should be placed upon using a sound, well-conceived activity coding structure that is separate from the activity identifier. Activities can be coded with more than one code for each activity, with each code holding a separate value, allowing outputs to be customized for different purposes. For example, codes can be used to identify project phases, subphases, location of work, project events, gates, significant accomplishments, sources of supply, source of design, the person or organization responsible to perform the activity, etc. These codes can be used alone or in multiple combinations. To achieve flexibility and enhanced functionality, most scheduling software supports multiple codes for each activity.

A structured activity numbering or identity scheme should form part of the overall coding design. The use of a structured activity identification system provides schedule users a better understanding of how a particular activity fits into the bigger project picture by grasping the significance of the activity identifier itself. For example, the identity scheme may even tie back to the project WBS. At a minimum, an activity identifier needs to be unique and follow a scheme appropriate to the project.

.9 Resource Planning

If the schedule model is to include resources of any type, the schedule model management plan identifies the elements required for resource planning and management. Items to consider are resource availability, resource calendars, and resource skill sets. Although resource loading of the schedule model is not required, this practice standard considers it a good practice and does recognize that resources should be considered by the project team when determining activity durations and activity sequencing. A resource-loaded schedule clearly indicates the interdependencies and impacts that the availability of resources will have on project duration and cost.

.10 Performance Indicators

To let the stakeholders know how the project is performing, many projects define key performance indicators (KPIs) enabling the project team to measure progress and performance toward predefined project goals (e.g., customer ratings/feedback, project team ratings, and EVM). EVM has the ability to combine measurements of scope, schedule, and cost in a single integrated system providing cost-based indicators. EVM can be expanded to include the concept of earned schedule, which has the objective of providing time-based indicators to complement cost-based indicators for project performance. For more information about EVM and earned schedule, refer to the *Practice Standard for Earned Value Management.*

.11 Master Schedule Model

The schedule model may be designed and built as a master project containing subprojects. The subprojects can be structured according to the various teams that comprise the project, such as phased execution (engineering, production, testing, and integration), globally distributed teams, or the contracting strategy (multiple projects, multiple project managers). These subprojects should be linked to each other in certain identified delivery/acceptance or interface points, ensuring that there is a connection among the plans. The schedule model management plan will define the steps used to create, manage, and control the master schedule, subprojects, and project interdependencies.

3.2 Schedule Model Creation

This section offers a general overview of the essential elements for developing a good schedule model. The good practices are shown for each component contained in the components list of this practice standard in Chapter 4. A review of Chapter 4 is strongly encouraged to understand all aspects associated with each component. It is crucial to take into consideration all of the information, procedures, and restrictions documented in the schedule model management section.

The purpose of the schedule model is to provide a useful detailed plan that can be used by the project manager and the project team to assist them in completing the project successfully. The schedule model becomes a tool developed by the project team that documents the team's vision of how the project will be performed. The schedule model includes when activities are supposed to start and finish, and is modified appropriately to reflect changes in progress, scope, etc., as they are added to the schedule model over the project life cycle. A well-developed schedule model is a dynamic tool that is used to provide a reasonable prediction of when the remaining project work can be expected to be accomplished. Simultaneously, it allows the project team to look at the performance of the project to date, and use that data to make accurate forecasts for the project evolutions that remain to be accomplished. Furthermore, once the project has been completed, the schedule model forms the basis for lessons learned activities and becomes the foundation for similar projects in the future.

The schedule model describes the work to be done (what), the resources required to do the work (who and what), and the optimum activity sequence including activity starts, finishes, and relationships (when). The way to do the work (how) is defined by other documents in the overall project plan. Establishing a realistic and achievable schedule model is one of the critical initial actions. Some important points to consider during the schedule model creation are:

- *Determine that the project requirements are understood and satisfied.* The project team reviews and understands the project's scope documents with particular emphasis given to the WBS. The project's scope documents provide the background, information, and understanding needed to develop the schedule model. The goal is to ensure that all aspects of the project execution have been adequately defined and included in the schedule model. Activities in the schedule model represent the work that produces the deliverables or work packages identified in the WBS; therefore, all work packages in the WBS should be directly traceable to a schedule activity or group of activities. Often the schedule activities can be organized to reflect the hierarchy of the WBS. Conversely, each activity should roll up into only one WBS element.

- *Verify resource availability and assignments.* The project team benefits greatly from a resource-loaded schedule. The workforce, material, equipment, and infrastructure needed to accomplish project activities can be planned in advance of need and anticipated problems can be mitigated. A basic schedule model produced for a project assumes that sufficient workforce and equipment are available to accomplish the activities as scheduled. This is not always the case because in a large or complex project, it may not be obvious that a resource deficiency exists. In the case of large and complex projects that involve multiple organizations and have a long duration, it may be required to include resources in the schedule model. See *PMBOK® Guide*—Fourth Edition for more information on resources. Just as activity codes can be used to classify and organize activities, resource codes (attributes) can be assigned to resources to classify resources according to organization, skill level or type, reporting structure, etc. In addition, resource IDs may be structured into a meaningful scheme, similar in nature to activity ID's.

3.2.1 Develop Schedule Model Baseline

The development of a good schedule model is achieved through the consistent application of sound general practices. Experience gained over time will assist in selecting appropriate responses to the design requirements for schedule model. The key steps include:

.1 Define Milestones

Once there is an understanding of the overall structure for the project data discussed previously, begin to lay out the project's milestones. Milestones will have zero duration, no resources assigned, will be used as benchmarks to measure progress, and may also reflect the start and finish points for various project events. Generally, a milestone will represent the start or completion of a portion or deliverable of the project and may also be associated with external constraints, such as the delivery of specific required permissions or equipment. Each project should have a start milestone and a finish milestone. The project will contain a list of milestones initially developed as the schedule model is created. These might have originated from the customer, team members or other stakeholders. As the schedule model is developed additional milestones are added as needed. It is an iterative process. (Note: Activities may be defined before milestones.)

.2 Design the Project's Activities

Begin to create the list of activities that will need to be performed to complete the project, based on the WBS and elaborated on by the team that will be responsible for the execution of the work. The characteristics of a well-designed activity include:

- The activity is a measurable and discrete element (or block) of work that is a tangible element of the project scope.

- A single person is responsible for the performance of the activity. This does not preclude the idea that multiple resources may be required to accomplish the activity, but it does require that a single entity is responsible for its performance. That person should be the same one who will report progress on the activity.

- Activities describe the work that needs to be accomplished. As such, the description for each activity starts with a verb and contains a unique, specific object. Although "pour wall" may be descriptive of a task, the activity description needs to be more specific. Adjectives may be helpful to clarify ambiguities. For example, "pour the east wall foundation from *x* to *y*" or "review Chapter 3 on terminology." Each activity description should be unique and leave no room for confusion, that is, it can be identified without ambiguity and it should be independent of the schedule presentation grouping or organization.

- The work represented by an activity, once started, should be capable of proceeding to completion without interruption (except for naturally occurring non-work periods in the calendar). If the work on an activity is suspended or delayed, it is often beneficial for the activity to be split into two or more activities at natural break points.

Typically, an activity's duration should be less than two times the update cycle. This allows the reporting of the start and finish of an activity within one or two update cycles, allowing management to focus on performance and corrective action if needed. Exceptions to this general rule are continuous activities (e.g., summary activities such as boring a 2-mile long tunnel or paving several miles of highway), procurement activities where a single work item (e.g., fabricating and shipping a component to a remote site) can take significantly longer than two update cycles, or a level-of-effort (LOE) activity such as administrative support. In these cases, the activity duration should simply reflect the anticipated time for the activity. Care needs to be given to LOE activities, because if they are given static durations equal to the length of the entire project, they may end up on or driving the critical path. By their very nature of supporting detailed work activities, LOE's cannot drive the project duration and cannot be critical. It is a good practice to define LOE activities in such a way that they will take their duration from the detailed activities that they support.

When completed, the activity list will describe 100% of the work required to complete the project, although not all activities necessarily need to be fully detailed if rolling wave planning is being used.

.3 Sequence Activities

Sequencing activities and milestones together with logic is the foundation of any schedule model. The method of connection is defined as a relationship. Every activity and milestone except the first (with no predecessor) and the last (with no successor) shall be connected to at least one predecessor and one successor. With the exception of the start milestone, something needs to occur prior to any activity starting, and in turn, that activity has to be totally or partially completed to allow another activity to start. Ensuring compliance with this practice will prevent the schedule from containing open ends, where activities or milestones are missing predecessors or successors, with the exception of the first and last milestones.

Typically, each predecessor activity would finish prior to the start of its successor activity (or activities) (known as a finish-to-start (FS) relationship). Sometimes it is necessary to overlap activities; an option may be selected to use start-to-start (SS), finish-to-finish (FF) or start-to-finish (SF) relationships. Figure 3-1 provides examples of the four relationship types in PDM (the most commonly used CPM methodology). Whenever possible, the FS logical relationship should be used. If other types of relationships are used, they should be used sparingly and with a full understanding of how the relationships have been implemented in the scheduling software being used. Ideally, the sequence of all activities will be defined in such a way that the start of every activity has a logical relationship from a predecessor and the finish of every activity has a logical relationship to a successor.

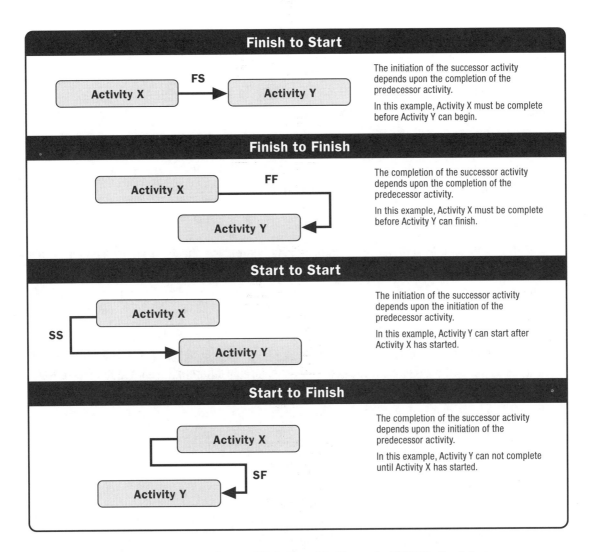

Figure 3-1. Illustrations of Relationship Types in CPM Methodology

Lag(s) may also be assigned to some relationships. A lag imposes a delay between the preceding and succeeding activity. For example, if an activity has a SS dependency with a lag of 15 days, it would delay the start of the successor activity until 5 days after the predecessor activity has started. The scheduler is cautioned to use lags with care and understand their impacts. Lags are only to be used to represent delays that are physically necessary, represent no work, and have duration. Some schedulers may be tempted to use lags to represent a period of time when work is actually occurring, such as review of a document before the next phase proceeds. It is recommended that these types of work be shown as activities in the schedule model instead of using a lag. When such activities are included, they could be coded to show that these are activities for which another party, for example the client, is responsible. This practice allows for better control of the project and makes it very visible if a specific entity is impacting the project.

Using more than one calendar in a schedule model may impact the calculated lag results within the schedule model. Additionally, understanding how different software packages utilize multiple calendars is extremely important.

It is also possible to assign constraints to activities and milestones that require the activity or milestone to start or finish at specific points in time. Study the various types of constraints that might be used and understand the effect and nuance their use has upon the schedule prior to use. The generally accepted practice is that constraints and lags should not be used to replace the addition of activities and relationships. However, as an example, utilization of constraints is generally acknowledged as necessary to meet contractual obligations.

In general, each activity should have an F-S or S-S predecessor and an F-S or F-F successor. Without these types of logical relationships the activities are called "dangling" and uncertainty in their durations will not necessarily be transmitted to the rest of the schedule model as they should be.

.4 Determine Resources for Each Activity

Estimate Activity Resources is the process of determining the type and quantities of material, personnel, equipment, or infrastructure required to perform each activity. If a project is constrained in terms of resources and the project duration could be impacted, resources should be incorporated into the schedule model. Although sometimes performed together, the Estimate Activity Resource process should be completed prior to Estimate Activity Durations (see *PMBOK® Guide*—Fourth Edition for more information). The hours needed for a senior designer to accomplish the activity versus a junior designer to perform the same activity could be considerably different, thus impacting the duration and quality of activity outputs and ultimately the cost of the project. On some projects, especially those of smaller scope, defining activities, sequencing activities, estimating resources, estimating activity durations, and developing the schedule model are so tightly linked that they are viewed as a single process. Resources can definitely impact the critical path if not considered by the project team.

.5 Determine the Duration for Each Activity

The duration is an estimate of how long it will take to accomplish the work involved in the activity. In many cases, the number of resources that are expected to be available to accomplish an activity, together with the productivity of those resources, may determine the activity's duration. A change to a driving resource allocated to the activity will have an effect on the duration, but this is not a simple "straight-line" relationship. Other factors influencing the duration are the type or skill level of the resources available to undertake the work, resource calendars, and the intrinsic nature of the work. Some activities (e.g., a 24-hour stress test) will take a set amount of time to complete regardless of the resource allocation.

While it is feasible to estimate a duration for an activity at any time, generally accepted good practice recommends defining the activity first, then tying it logically into the overall schedule sequence and then focusing on activity resources and duration. At this time, the relationship between the activity duration and work in the schedule will be more easily understood; so resource flows, activity team sizes, and the like can begin to be determined. The relationship between the activity's duration and cost will be made explicit in the basis of estimate or assumptions for both the cost and the schedule. This document should be kept current as schedule durations change during schedule model maintenance. See Section 3.3 on Schedule Model Maintenance as well as Section 3.4 on Schedule Model Analysis for more information.

It is important to understand the method used by the schedule model in order to plan the activities related to duration estimation for each schedule activity. The method used can imply a deterministic or probabilistic schedule. Deterministic schedule models are networks of activities connected with dependencies which describe the work to be performed, static duration, and the planned date to complete the project if everything goes according to plan. Probabilistic schedule models are networks with all elements of a deterministic schedule model, but the activity duration of the tasks are random variables. For more information about estimating activity duration, please refer to the *Practice Standard for Project Estimating.* For more information on the best practices for project risk analysis using probabilistic schedule models, see the *Practice Standard for Risk Management.*

.6 Analyze the Schedule Output

Once completed, the schedule model will contain a set of unique activities, having varying durations, connected by defined logical relationships. It provides the project team with information on what needs to be accomplished and the sequence required to accomplish the project deliverables. However, it still does not indicate when these various activities should be performed. In order to acquire that information, the scheduling tool is activated to calculate the dates and other values within the schedule model according to the chosen scheduling method. Despite the speed of many computer programs, the scheduling function always requires three distinct processes for time analysis and a fourth process, if resource smoothing or leveling is being used. The discrete steps are:

- A start date is assigned to the start milestone. Then, moving throughout the network from activity to activity (from left to right) and in the sequence defined by the logical relationships, start and finish dates are assigned to each activity and milestone, as determined by the defined durations. This is called the forward pass. The start and finish dates on each activity are called the early start and early finish dates, and when the analysis reaches the end of the network, it establishes the earliest possible finish date for the project and the shortest project duration based on the activity estimated durations and logical relationships as defined.

- Next, a finish date is assigned to the end milestone. This could be the same date as the one calculated by the forward pass or a different date applied as a constraint. The analysis process then works back through the network from right to left until it arrives back at the start milestone, and another set of start and finish dates is assigned to each activity. This is called the backward pass and establishes the late start and late finish dates for each activity and milestone.

- Float values are calculated by comparing the early and late dates as follows:

  o *Total float* is calculated by subtracting the early finish date from the late finish date (or the early start from the late start). Negative total float means dates are not feasible without changing the plan.

  o *Free float* is calculated by subtracting the early finish date of the activity from the early start of the earliest of its successors. Free float is never a negative value.

- Once the float values have been calculated, resource leveling may be carried out to minimize resource over allocations or reduce the fluctuations in resource demand. If this process is to be done automatically, the scheduler needs to determine the processes and algorithms to be used. Most project scheduling software packages have multiple options and settings that can have a significant impact on the resulting resource leveled schedule. Regardless of what settings the scheduling software has, there will most likely be a trade-off between allowing the leveling solution to extend the project total duration and allowing the use of more resources than allowed initially. The resources leveled in one area could be over allocated in other areas. A complete view of resource allocation across all activities must be reviewed before finalizing the resource leveling. Some may be tempted to do the resource leveling manually by adjusting the logic or adding constraints to delay the start of certain activities; this is not a good practice as it interferes with the normal scheduling calculation.

.7 Approve the Schedule

The project team should be actively involved in reviewing the results of this initial scheduling process. The review should consider the analyzed project end date, milestone completion dates, critical paths (the longest path for the project or as constraint driven), total float values and resource requirements (compared to resource availability) to determine the acceptability of the schedule. Where alterations are required, changes are made to the schedule logic, resource allocations, and/or durations, and then the schedule is reanalyzed. The most common alteration required involves actions to reduce the overall duration of the schedule. The key techniques used to compress the schedule are crashing and fast tracking. Crashing consists essentially of adding resources to critical activities to shorten their durations while fast tracking consists of changing the logic by overlapping critical activities rather than working them strictly in sequence. Crashing only works for activities that are effort driven where adding resources will reduce the activity's duration."

Crashing typically increases project costs by some factor while fast tracking increases the risk of rework as activities are started before their initial predecessors are completed. (see also Chapter 6 of the *PMBOK® Guide*—Fourth Edition). These iterations continue until an acceptable schedule model is developed—one that the key project stakeholders can agree is attainable. The formal process for the approval of the baseline schedule model will be defined in the schedule model management plan.

.8 Baseline the Schedule Model

Once agreed upon, the first version of the schedule that is developmentally complete to be approved for capture or copied for future reference is called the project baseline schedule model. This baseline becomes the benchmark against which project performance may be measured. It is a generally accepted practice that every project has a baseline schedule model in place before the execution of the project work. Once the baseline has been approved through formal procedures, reports are distributed in accordance with the project's communication plan and changes to the baseline are monitored and controlled through the integrated change control process.

3.3 Schedule Model Maintenance

Most every project will inevitably experience changes. To ensure successful project execution, effective change control and disciplined maintenance procedures are necessary. The key is to determine how the project will approve and track changes as they occur throughout the project's life cycle. Change can occur simply by work progressing more quickly or slowly than planned, as well as when changes in other elements of the project occur (e.g., scope changes) and/or whether the project team decides to modify its approach to the project work.

Tracking progress begins after the project model is baselined, work begins, and regular monitoring and controlling processes are implemented. These processes are important to help identify problems as early as possible, minimizing their impact on the successful completion of the project. The main steps for tracking progress are as follows:

- Saving a baseline schedule model, which contains the dates against which progress is compared. The current schedule model may be copied and approved as a baseline, or a more suitable schedule model may be approved as a baseline.

- Schedule progress is reported as of a specific data date, also known as status date, update date, current date, time now date, or as-of-date. This progress, as a minimum, should include actual start and actual finish dates, remaining durations, and percent completes.

- Assigning the new data date and recalculating all the activity dates are the last steps for progressing the schedule model.

The status/update process occurs on a regular basis determined during the project planning process. The steps involved in maintaining the schedule at each status/update are described in 3.3.1 through 3.3.7.

3.3.1   Collect Actuals and Remaining Work

Collect the actual status of the work at predetermined time intervals for the project. The information collected includes the actual start dates for all activities that have commenced and actual finish dates for all activities that have been completed as of the data date. Where an activity is in progress, the amount of work accomplished and the time needed to complete the remaining work is determined. Status collection also includes changes in durations for future activities. Other information gathered at this time may include data on resource utilization and costs incurred. The data is collected as of a nominated data date (date/time). This data date is analogous to "time now" in earned value performance management (EVPM).

3.3.2   Update and Progress the Schedule Model According to the Actuals

Enter status information into the schedule model and reanalyze the remaining work to determine the project status. All incomplete work will be rescheduled to a date/time equal to or later than the data date. Care should be taken, as many software tools allow actual dates to be applied to future work. Quality control practices should be in place to identify the entry of actual dates beyond the data date and percent complete values being reported that are not valid in relation to the dates.

3.3.3   Compare and Resolve Any Deviation

Compare the newly updated schedule model outputs with the stored baseline and manage cost and schedule variances. Variance thresholds defined in the schedule model management plan may be used to determine which activities and conditions require reporting and further action. A commonly used date variance is the finish variance between early finish and baseline finish, which is usually expressed in units such as working days. Comparing the status of an activity against more than one target may be useful; for example, current schedule vs.:

- The original plan—the baseline—to see the slippage compared to the original plan.

- The last update period to see the changes since the last update.

3.3.4   Update the Schedule Model with Approved Changes

Update the schedule model with any approved changes resulting from the overall change control process to ensure the schedule model represents 100% of the current work scope of the project. The updating and adjustment processes may need a number of iterations to maintain a schedule model that remains realistic and achievable.

3.3.5   Update the Baseline Schedule Model

Update, per the formal change control process, the baseline schedule model if authorized scope changes have been incorporated into the updated schedule model, or if other changes have been incorporated that significantly change the nature of project execution. Only the activities that are new or approved for change, and those activities that are directly or indirectly linked to them, should be rebaselined.

3.3.6   Communicate

Distribute reports (schedule model presentations, see Figures 2-1 and 2-7) in accordance with the schedule model management plan and the project communications management plan once the current schedule update cycle has been completed.

3.3.7   Maintain the Records

Proper record management is part of configuration control. Properly maintained records that detail the initial logic and major decision points of the project and the thought process that went into creating the baselined schedule flow logic aids in defense of actions taken and lessons learned. Maintain records that explain all changes in activity durations or logic as the alterations are being made in the schedule model. Activity log notes are often used for this purpose. These records will provide valuable data if it becomes necessary to reconstruct what happened and why.

Many of the good practices and elements described previously are also included within the details of each component contained within the schedule model components list as presented in Chapter 4. A complete understanding of the various components is needed in order to maximize the potential for their proper application and the development of a sound schedule.

3.4 Schedule Model Analysis

Schedule analysis utilizes common tools and techniques throughout the project life cycle in order to identify deviation from the baseline schedule model. Schedule analysis is the responsibility of the project team and the primary objective of the analysis is the early identification of threats and opportunities to the project objectives.

There are several tools and techniques available to perform schedule model analysis. The specific procedures and policies to be used for a project are described in the project's schedule management plan. The most common items reviewed during schedule analysis are described in 3.4.1 through 3.4.11.

3.4.1 Critical Path and Critical Activities

.1 Critical Path

The critical path is typically, but not always, the sequence of the schedule activities that predicts or defines the longest duration of the project. Generally, it is the longest path through the project and therefore determines the duration of the project. However, a critical path can end, as an example, on a schedule milestone that is in the middle of the schedule model and that has a finish-no-later-than date constraint. (Remember that constraints are to be used selectively in schedule models.) But risk(s) and constraint(s) can alter the critical path, elevating the importance of seemingly lesser activities and causing unexpected changes to project duration and cost. A project can have multiple critical paths. A project with multiple critical paths has a higher level of risk since the failure to meet any of these might result in failure to complete all project milestones.

.2 Critical Activities

It is important to distinguish between critical path activities and critical activities. Critical path activities are those activities contained in the critical path(s). Critical activities are those activities vital to the success of the project, even if they are not on the CPM predicted critical path or critical chain. Critical activities are normally high risk in terms of scope, schedule, and cost and can cause not only a delay in the project end date, but an increased likelihood of project failure. All activities in the critical path are also considered critical activities. The critical path calculations consider activities and constraints to determine the longest path in the project. Critical activities can be outside the critical path.

3.4.2 Total Float and Free Float

Free float represents the amount of time an activity CPM early finish date may be delayed without impacting any successor activities' CPM early start date. Total float represents the amount of time an activity CPM early start date or CPM early finish date may be delayed without impacting the CPM late finish date of the entire project or violating a schedule model constraint date. Review each activity total float and free float to determine if they have changed since the previous update. Changes to total float indicate a threat of achieving project completion or specific milestones; free float indicates how lack of progress impacts immediate successors. Total float and free float may be reduced by external dependencies and other hard constraint dates listed in the schedule model. These external dependencies should be explained in activity nodes or linked to external milestones.

Monitoring and managing these two vital components are critical to completing the project on time and meeting milestones as planned. Decreases to total float and free float indicate where recovery plans need to be developed.

3.4.3   Level of Effort Activities (LOE)

Level-of-effort (LOE) activities are to support other work activities or the entire project effort. Examples of such an activity may be project management, project budget accounting, customer liaison, or rotating machinery during storage (preventive maintenance), etc.

Since an LOE activity is not itself a work item directly associated with accomplishing the final project product, service, or result, but rather one that supports such work, its duration is based on the duration of the discrete work activities that it is supporting. For example, when providing security forces to staff the entrance to the work site, they will start when the works begins and end when the project is finished. As a result, an LOE activity should never be on the critical path of the schedule model, as it never adds time to the project. Rather, machinery installation would be on the critical path, and the preventive maintenance activity would become shorter or longer only if machinery time-in-storage does. When inserting LOE activities into a critical path method schedule, the LOE is usually scheduled as both a start-to-start (SS) and finish-to-finish (FF) successor of the driving activities. In a network logic diagram, these two relationships make it appear as though the LOE is hanging from the start and finish of the discrete activity. As a result, an LOE diagrammed in this manner is sometimes referred to as a hammock activity. A hammock activity is a bridging activity, using SS and FF relationships to supporting activities, or in the case of LOE, activities that it supports. LOE activity, unlike hammock activities, may have any type of relationship, like hammocks they are not confined to SS and FF relationships. They may have many types of relationships associated with them. Resource leveling may not be performed and constraints may not be applied on LOEs; they use their assigned calendars to summarize their dates.

3.4.4   Probabilistic Distribution of Activity Durations

If activity durations involve a great deal of uncertainty, a commonly used estimating technique is the three-point estimate. These three points correspond to activity duration defined as optimistic, most likely, and pessimistic durations. Additionally, the risk register may also be used to support estimating the uncertainty in activity durations. In order to quantify uncertainty about the overall project duration, starting from the three-point estimate of every activity, PERT (which uses an approximation of beta distribution, and the equation in Section 2.2.3) can be utilized. The activity optimistic duration and activity pessimistic duration represent the probable durations, but not the entire domain of values. The three-point estimates of duration should be made by those performing the activities or by someone with experience performing similar activities. The most common approach for creating the probabilistic distribution is to estimate the most likely value as accurately as possible and then to skew the distribution toward maximum or minimum values. The degree to which the distribution is skewed is suggested by the shape of a curve fitting the three estimated durations (such as beta, uniform, or triangular). The distribution relating the three duration estimates (or cost estimates) should be selected to best fit the supporting data for similar activities.

3.4.5 Schedule Risk

Schedule risk analysis is utilized to establish and validate schedule contingencies, identify priority risks and risk-driven events, and continuously monitor changes on project-related risks. PERT does not recognize that parallel float paths can contribute to risk especially at merge points also known as "merge bias" or "path convergence." It is too complex to perform a deep analysis of this bias without doing a simulation such as Monte Carlo simulation which will determine magnitude of the bias. The larger and more complex a project, the greater the cumulative impact of risk on the project. The circumstances dictating the frequency, rigor, and use of schedule risk analysis are documented in the project management plan or other contractual documents. For more information on risk concepts see the *Practice Standard for Project Risk Management.*

3.4.6 Date Constraints

Date constraints restrict a project's natural flow, disregard the effects of risk, and limit the usefulness of schedule risk analysis. Date constraints should be avoided whenever possible and used only when compatible with a project's expected course of development. For example, one use of a date constraint might be to establish a not-earlier-than or a not-later-than date for activities for which there is no effective predecessor or successor in the schedule. An illustrative example may be delivery of a piece of equipment by a vendor where it is not practical or desirable to include the vendor's activities in the schedule model. Even in this example, care should be taken so as not to inject a break in the critical path. Constraints can be flexible (e.g., as soon as possible), moderately flexible (e.g., finish no earlier than) or inflexible (e.g., must start on). Moderately flexible constraints are sometimes called soft constraints and inflexible constraints are sometimes called hard constraints. Since constraints limit scheduling flexibility, they should be used only when schedule logic cannot correctly address the situation. When a date constraint becomes necessary, flexible constraints are preferred over inflexible constraints.

3.4.7 Open-Ended Activities

An open-ended activity is an activity lacking either a predecessor or a successor or both. Open-ended activities can obscure the logical relationships between project activities, create a false appearance of float in a project, and reduce the apparent impact of risk during a schedule analysis. The only open-ended activities in a project should be the start and finish milestones at the beginning and end of the project. Unless linked to other projects, a project's start and finish milestones will always contain open ends.

3.4.8 Out of Sequence (OOS) Logic

OOS logic arises when a project is already in progress. An activity may be reported as started before its predecessor is reported as finished, causing OOS logic. For example, if Activity A has a finish-to-start (FS) relationship with Activity B, but Activity B has been updated with an actual start date before Activity A has been updated with an actual finish date, the result is OOS logic. OOS logic should be corrected (e.g., by further decomposition of Activity A) or removed in order to preserve the integrity of the risk analysis. Schedule analysis will properly identify how to best resolve OOS logic problems; however, do not rely solely on the scheduling tool to correct the problem, because only the team can best determine the OOS logic resolution. In some cases, it may be that the defined relationship created during the planning stage was not correct and should be corrected for this project and for future reference.

3.4.9 Leads and Lags

Risk can consume or extend fixed lags with unanticipated consequences to overall project duration. Leads and lags can introduce schedule risk and should be modeled as discrete activities with their own duration uncertainty whenever possible. Leads can also introduce cost risk especially in JIT (just-in-time) inventory management; this, in turn, may have a cascading effect on the schedule model if the project is being managed with a limited inventory space. Expressing leads/lags as discrete activities is required if Monte Carlo simulation software does not allow assignment of duration uncertainty to a lead/lag. Additionally, promoting a lead/lag to a full activity allows it to be assigned with additional attributes, such as a name, remaining duration, etc. The lack of visibility of the lead/lag and the distortion of the critical path calculation contribute to schedule risk. There is specific risk associated with any leads and lags applied to activities where different calendars (activity or resource) are in use. Therefore, it is important to have a clear understanding of the consequences that leads and lags can have on a schedule model. Many software tools may allow leads and lags to be defined as either fixed duration or as a percentage of the activity duration; judgment is needed to use the correct method best representing the nature of the activity and the lead or lag.

3.4.10 Start-to-Finish Relationship

Start-to-finish (SF) relationships are seldom deliberately used in deterministic planning because they involve the unusual circumstance of a successor task happening before its logical predecessor. Review any SF relationship to ensure that it is not the result of scheduling errors and modify them if necessary. The following illustrative example of a SF relationship provides a better understanding of this rare relationship:

> *Example*—Assume that the project requires the delivery of a piece of equipment to support construction activities. It may not be practical to provide logic for the equipment fabrication and delivery activities, yet the team wants the construction activities to drive the dates of the delivery. Since the predecessor always drives the successor, the SF relationship provides the solution. Then the equipment fabrication may conclude upon the start of the activity requiring the equipment to be installed.

3.4.11 Links to/from Summary Activities

It generally is not recommended to use links on summary activities because the logic can be difficult to follow and the practice may not be supported by all scheduling tools. Use of links on summary activities may produce logic errors and create circular logic within the schedule model.

3.5 Communication and Reporting

Clear communications build credibility with the stakeholders. The project manager along with the project team should create a communication management plan (see *PMBOK® Guide*—Fourth Edition) early in the project life cycle to meet the identified expectations of the key stakeholders.

The schedule model is a strategic and important element in a project manager's toolset for guiding a project successfully to its target completion date. A schedule model is a timeline or calendar that lists activities with expected start and finish dates. A schedule model also can be layered with different details to enable project managers to direct and manage resources more smoothly, control the day to day project evolutions, communicate more frequently and effectively with stakeholders, and identify and monitor dependencies and constraints between tasks to minimize the impact to the project for preventable delays.

The schedule model instance can produce multiple report formats depending upon the purpose of the schedule model, the stage of the development of the project, and the primary user of the schedule model. Customers may require various levels of schedule model instance presentations. For more information see the component "schedule model level" in Chapter 4.

Table 3-1. Levels of Schedule Model Instance Presentations

Level	Recipient	Content	Example
1	Executive Management and Sponsor	Key information only	Project start and finish dates and cost
2	Project Management and Project Team	Key project milestones	Progress of all project milestones
3	Project Coordinators	Summary tasks	Needs to provide sufficient information to define the project scope of work for each group, control the progress and forecast deliverables
4	Work Package Managers or Contract Managers	Detailed information by each work package	Similar to level 3 except that the data is segregated by contract or work package
5	Task Leaders	Detailed information by task	Detailed project schedule data

CHAPTER 4

SCHEDULING COMPONENTS

The following section provides a detailed cataloging of the potential components of a scheduling tool. Each entry includes eight possible types of information related to each component, and indicates whether the component is considered to be required, conditional, or optional by this practice standard. Required components are divided into four groups: Core Required Components (CRC, shown as "R" in the tables), Resource Required Components (RRC), EVM Required Components (ERC) and Risk Required Components (KRC). The requirements of the project determine which required components need to be present in a schedule model before a maturity assessment can be performed. The maturity assessment and conformance index are explained in detail in Chapter 5. This chapter is divided into the following sections:

4.1 How to Use the Components List. This section defines the type of information that can be shown for each component.

4.2 List of Components by Category. This section depicts a breakdown of the components within a specific category. This information will make it easier to locate a specific component. Each component is identified as required, conditional, or optional.

4.3 Detailed Components List. This section lists each schedule component and its associated types of information in alphabetical order.

4.1 How to Use the Components List

The layout for a typical component entry is shown below. The subsections of 4.1 define the content for each data element within the component item.

Component Name / Required, Conditional or Optional Use / Manual or Calculated

Data Format:

Behavior:

Good Practices:

Conditional Note/Associated Component:

Definition:

4.1.1   Component Name

This data element contains the name of the component within a scheduling tool, which may differ within a selected tool. The other attributes should be the same so that familiarity with the standard will allow for proper usage.

4.1.2   Required, Conditional or Optional Use

This data element indicates whether the use of a component is: required, for any schedule model; conditionally required, based on the state or action of another component or a process; or optional.

4.1.3   Manual or Calculated

This data element indicates whether the data within the component is manually entered or calculated by the scheduling tool. The manual/calculated attribute setting is schedule-tool dependent.

4.1.4   Data Format

This data element describes how data is formatted within the component as part of the scheduling tool. The data format may vary between scheduling tools.

4.1.5   Behavior

In the components list, this data element describes how the component reacts and/or enables reaction within the scheduling tool. It is important to note that all of the behavior descriptions start with a verb indicating the action. The actual behavior of a component may vary between scheduling tools or settings within the same tool.

4.1.6   Good Practices

In this list, "good practices" means that there is general agreement that the correct application of skills, tools, and techniques, when applied in conjunction with the named component, can enhance the chances of success over a wide range of different projects. Good practice does not mean that the knowledge described should always be applied uniformly on all projects. The project management team is responsible for determining what is appropriate for any given project.

4.1.7   Conditional Note/Associated Component

This data element indicates whether this component's action is dependent on the state or action of another component.

4.1.8   Definition

This data element describes the overall use and function of the component within the scheduling tool. The definition provided is the same as provided in the Glossary, where applicable.

4.2 List of Components by Category

This section contains a list of the components organized by categories. The Use column identifies whether a component is a core required component (R), resource required component (RRC), Earned Value Management required component (ERC), risk required component (KRC), optional (O), or not scored (NS). All of the required components shall be present to achieve a score on the maturity assessment process described in greater detail in Chapter 5.

Table 4-1. List of Components by Category

Category	Component	Use	Category	Component	Use
CALENDAR	Project Calendar	R	RELATIONSHIP	Finish to Finish	O
	Activity Calendar	O		Finish to Start	R
	Resource Calendar	RRC		Start to Finish	NS
CONSTRAINT	As Late As Possible	NS		Start to Start	O
	As Soon As Possible	NS	RESOURCE	Activity Effort/Work	O
	Expected Finish	NS		Activity Resource Actual Quantity	RRC
	Finish Not Earlier Than	NS		Activity Resource Total Quantity	RRC
	Finish Not Later Than	O		Driving Resources	O
	Finish On	NS		Project Resource Actual Quantity	RRC
	Mandatory Finish Date	NS		Project Resource Total Quantity	RRC
	Mandatory Start Date	NS		Resource Assignment	RRC
	Project Finish Constraint	O		Resource Availability	RRC
	Project Start Constraint	O		Resource Description	RRC
	Start Not Earlier Than	NS		Resource ID	RRC
	Start Not Later Than	NS		Resource Lag	O
	Start On	NS		Resource Leveling	O
DURATION	Activity Actual Duration	R		Resource Library/Dictionary	RRC
	Activity Original Duration	R		Resource Rates/Prices	O
	Activity Remaining Duration	R		Resource Type	RRC
	Activity Total Duration	R	SCHEDULE RISK	Activity Cumulative Probability Risk Distribution	KRC
	Project Actual Duration	R		Activity Most Likely Duration	KRC
	Project Remaining Duration	R		Activity Optimistic Duration	KRC
	Project Total Duration	R		Activity Pessimistic Duration	KRC
EARNED VALUE	Activity Actual Cost	ERC		Activity Risk Criticality Index	KRC
	Budget At Completion (BAC)	ERC		Risk ID	KRC
	Change Request Identifier	O		Probability Risk Distribution	KRC
	Control Account ID	ERC	START DATE	Activity Actual Start Date	R
	Control Account Manager (CAM)	O		Activity Early Start Date	R
	Cost Performance Index (CPI)	O		Activity Late Start Date	R
	Cost Variance % (CV%)	O		Activity Resource Leveled Start Date	O
	Cost Variance (CV)	O		Project Actual Start Date	R
	Earned Value (EV)	ERC		Project Early Start Date	R
	Earned Value Method	O		Project Late Start Date	R
	Earned Value Weight	O		Project Resource Leveled Start Date	O
	Estimate at Completion (EAC)	ERC	MISCELLA-NEOUS	Activity Code	O
	Estimate to Completion (ETC)	ERC		Activity Cost Category	O
	Planned Value	ERC		Activity Cost Estimate	O
	Schedule Performance Index (SPI)	O		Activity ID	R
	Schedule Variance % (SV%)	O		Activity Label	R
	Schedule Variance (SV)	O		Activity Scope Definition	O
	To Complete Performance Index (TCPI)	O		Baseline Schedule Model	R
	WBS ID	ERC		Critical Path	R
	Work Package Identifier	ERC		Custom Field	O
FINISH DATE	Activity Actual Finish Date	R		Data Date	R
	Activity Early Finish Date	R		Lag	O
	Activity Late Finish Date	R		Lead	NS
	Activity Resource Leveled Finish Date	O		Milestones	R
	Project Actual Finish Date	R		Project Cost Category	O
	Project Early Finish Date	R		Project Description	O
	Project Late Finish Date	R		Project Manager	O
	Project Resource Leveled Finish Date	O		Project Name	R
FLOAT	Free Float	R		Project Schedule Level	O
	Total Float	R		Presentation	R
PERCENT COMPLETE	Activity Physical % Complete OR Activity Duration % Complete	R		Schedule Model ID	R
				Schedule Model Version	R
	Activity Work Percent Complete	O		Summary Activity	O
	Project Physical % Complete OR Project Duration % Complete	R		Target Schedule Model	O
				Unit of Measure	R
				Variance	O

4.3 Detailed Components List

This section identifies individual components and the eight types of information defined for each component. It is organized alphabetically.

Activity Actual Cost (AC)	Required (ERC)	Calculated

Data Format: Number
Behavior: Measurement of cost
Good Practices: Include actual cost when using earned value methodology in the schedule.
Conditional Note/Associated Component: See the *Practice Standard for Earned Value Management*. This term is also known as actual cost of work performed (ACWP). This standard recognizes AC may only be available at summarized levels of activities and not for each discrete activity in the schedule model.
Definition: The total cost of the work completed during a given time period. This value may be calculated at any schedule model outline level and between various data dates. If the calculation is performed using the project start date and the most current data date, the values are called "cumulative."

Activity Actual Duration	Required	Calculated/Manual

Data Format: Numeric
Behavior: Defines the length of time that has elapsed since the activity began. The unit of measure may be elapsed time or work time.
Good Practices:
Conditional Note/Associated Component:
Definition: The total number of work periods in calendar units between the activity actual start date of the schedule activity and either the data date of the schedule model, if the schedule activity is in progress, or the activity actual finish date, if the schedule activity is complete.

Activity Actual Finish Date	Required	Manual

Data Format: Date
Behavior: Defines the date that the activity was completed.
Good Practices: All activities with finishes prior to the data date should have actual finish dates assigned. Actual dates replace CPM early and late dates. Specifies that the activity is 100% complete.
Conditional Note/Associated Component: Percent Complete
Definition: The point in time at which a scheduled activity is completed.

Activity Actual Start Date	Required	Manual

Data Format: Date
Behavior: Defines progress having been initiated on an activity.
Good Practices: Actual dates need to be assigned to all actual starts prior to the data date. Actual dates replace CPM early and late dates.
Conditional Note/Associated Component: Progress needs to have been initiated prior to the current data date.
Definition: The point in time at which a schedule activity began.

Activity Calendar	Optional	Manual

Data Format: Date/Time

Behavior: Defines the working periods for the activity. The activity calendar overrides the project calendar for those activities to which it is applied.

Good Practices:

Conditional Note/Associated Component:

Definition: A calendar of working and non-working periods assigned to the schedule activity which defines the work periods and non-work periods in calendar format. The activity calendar, on the schedule activities to which it is assigned, is used to replace the project calendar for calculations during schedule calculations. See also *project calendar* and *resource calendar*.

Activity Code	Optional	Manual

Data Format: Alphanumeric

Behavior: Indicates the classification of the task/activity

Good Practices: Activity codes should be used to facilitate sorting, organizing, summarizing, and grouping.

Conditional Note/Associated Component:

Definition: One or more numerical or text values that identify characteristics of the work or in some way categorize the schedule activity that allows filtering and ordering of activities within reports.

Activity Cost Category	Optional	Manual

Data Format: Alphanumeric.

Behavior: Provides additional breakdowns that can be assigned for a specific cost account within the project.

Good Practices: For accounting purposes, costs should be broken down into categories, such as direct, indirect, labor, material, equipment, etc.

Conditional Note/Associated Component:

Definition: A breakdown of the cost, such as labor cost, equipment cost, and material cost.

Activity Cost Estimate	Optional	Manual

Data Format: Numeric

Behavior: Derived by adding all individual activity cost categories. May include costs in addition to those included in the planned value (PV).

Good Practices: The activity costs should be calculated by adding the individual activity cost categories that have been assigned to the activity.

Conditional Note/Associated Component: Activity cost category, planned value

Definition: The projected cost of the schedule activity, which includes the cost for all resources required to perform and complete the activity, including all cost types and cost categories.

Activity Cumulative Probability Risk Distribution   Required (KRC)   Manual

Data Format: Table of dates, numeric (fractional)

Behavior: Stores results of method used to quantify uncertainty based upon the chosen probability distribution function representing risk of activity durations.

Good Practices: The risk analysis process should be used for projects where schedule variances could have a significant impact on project objectives.

Conditional Note/Associated Component:

Definition: A table of dates and their associated cumulative probabilities of occurrence for schedule activity completion. Dates are derived using analytical techniques such as Monte Carlo calculations. When applied to the project end date, the value is equivalent to the project cumulative probability risk distribution.

Activity Duration Percent Complete   Required (see Activity Physical Percent Complete)   Calculated/Manual

Data Format: Numeric (fractional)

Behavior: Represents the proportion of actual duration as a percentage of total expected activity duration completed at a given point in time.

Good Practices: In the absence of earned value management, duration percent complete may be used as an indication of activity progress. However, users need to recognize that this is a very rough approximation of true progress, and its use in lieu of EVM is discouraged. It is the percent complete of the span of the activity without relation to the amount of work effort for the activity.

Conditional Note/Associated Component: Shall use either activity duration percent complete or activity physical percent complete.

Definition: The calculated percentage that the activity actual duration is of the activity total duration for a schedule activity that has work in progress.

Activity Early Finish Date   Required   Calculated

Data Format: Date

Behavior: Identifies the early finish date of the activity, based on the CPM forward pass.

Good Practices: Date will be derived from the CPM calculations.

Conditional Note/Associated Component: Early start, duration

Definition: The earliest possible point in time when the uncompleted portion of the schedule activity can be completed given the assigned resources.

Activity Early Start Date   Required   Calculated

Data Format: Date

Behavior: Defines the early start of the activity, based on the CPM forward pass.

Good Practices: Derived from the schedule network analysis calculations.

Conditional Note/Associated Component:

Definition: The earliest possible point in time when the schedule activity can begin based on the CPM forward pass of schedule model logic.

Activity Effort/Work	Optional	Manual

Data Format: Numeric

Behavior: Quantifies labor units required for an activity.

Good Practices: Resources should be identified and assigned. If a labor resource is identified, effort is assigned.

Conditional Note/Associated Component: Depends on activity duration and resource assignment.

Definition: The number of labor units required to complete a schedule activity or work breakdown structure component. Activity effort is usually expressed as staff hours, staff days, or staff weeks. Not the same as duration.

Activity ID	Required	Calculated

Data Format: Alphanumeric

Behavior: Identifies the schedule activity.

Good Practices: A unique identifier which can be automatically generated or follows a numbering scheme appropriate for the project. Many projects assign a reasoned structure or "coding" to the activity ID.

Conditional Note/Associated Component:

Definition: A short unique numeric or text identification assigned to each schedule activity to differentiate that project activity from other activities. The activity ID is typically unique within any one schedule model network diagram.

Activity Label	Required	Manual

Data Format: Alphanumeric

Behavior: Allows user-defined information to be recorded about the activity.

Good Practices: Phrase or label starting with a verb and a unique, specific subject (noun/adjective).

Conditional Note/Associated Component:

Definition: A short phrase or label for each schedule activity used in conjunction with an activity identifier to differentiate that schedule model activity from other schedule activities. The activity description normally describes the scope of work of the schedule activity. Also known as activity name, task name.

Activity Late Finish Date	Required	Calculated

Data Format: Date

Behavior: Identifies the late finish of the activity based on the CPM backward pass.

Good Practices: Derived from the CPM calculations.

Conditional Note/Associated Component:

Definition: The latest possible point in time when the schedule activity can be completed without violating a schedule constraint or delaying the project end date.

Activity Late Start Date　　　　　Required　　　　　Calculated

Data Format:　　Date
Behavior:　Defines the late start of the activity, based on the backwards pass.
Good Practices:　Derived from the CPM calculations.
Conditional Note/Associated Component:
Definition:　The latest possible point in time when the schedule activity can begin without violating a schedule constraint or delaying the project end date.

Activity Most Likely Duration　　　　　Required (KRC)　　　　　Manual

Data Format:　　Numeric
Behavior:　Identifies the length of time allocated to complete the schedule activity assuming normal conditions. Risks are only calculated on remaining durations.
Good Practices:　Most likely durations should be used for schedule risk calculations.
Conditional Note/Associated Component:
Definition:　The total number of work periods in calendar units assigned to perform the schedule activity, considering all of the variables that could affect performance; it is determined to be the most probable activity duration.

Activity Optimistic Duration　　　　　Required (KRC)　　　　　Manual

Data Format:　　Numeric
Behavior:　Identifies the length of time allocated to complete the schedule activity assuming the best possible conditions. Risks are only calculated on remaining durations.
Good Practices:　Optimistic durations should be used for schedule risk calculations.
Conditional Note/Associated Component:
Definition:　The total number of work periods in calendar units assigned to perform the schedule activity, considering all of the variables that could affect performance; it is determined to be the shortest possible activity duration.

Activity Original Duration　　　　　Required　　　　　Manual

Data Format:　　Numeric
Behavior:　Defines the length of time allocated to complete the schedule activity prior to reporting any progress on the activity. The implementation of activity original duration are scheduling tool dependent.
Good Practices:　A record should be maintained of how the duration was determined for future reference and revisions. Generally, durations should not exceed two or three reporting cycles.
Conditional Note/Associated Component:
Definition:　The activity duration originally assigned to a schedule activity; this duration is typically not updated as progress is reported on the activity. Used for comparison with activity actual duration and activity remaining duration when reporting schedule progress, the activity original duration is normally developed with a reliance on historic data, specialists, resource availability, financial considerations, and volume of work to be performed.

Activity Pessimistic Duration	Required (KRC)	Manual

Data Format: Numeric
Behavior: Identifies the length of time allocated to complete the schedule activity assuming the worst possible conditions. Risks are only calculated on remaining durations.
Good Practices: Most likely durations should be used for schedule risk calculations.
Conditional Note/Associated Component: Resource assignments may impact activity remaining duration.
Definition: The total number of work periods in calendar units assigned to perform the schedule activity, considering all of the variables that could affect performance; it is determined to be the longest possible activity duration.

Activity Physical Percent Complete	Required (see Activity Duration Percent Complete)	Manual

Data Format: Numeric (fractional)
Behavior: Represents the proportion of actual physical work as a percentage of total expected physical work completed at a given point in time.
Good Practices: For any started activity, the physical percent complete needs to be updated. The project scheduler should make a decision at the beginning of the project as to which method will be used for the duration of the project. There may be different methods to measure completeness. These include the earned value-based earning rules (see Practice Standard for EVM) such as 50/50 rule, actual quantities, percent complete, non-linear by milestone, etc., as well as estimates by the people working the activity. Of these methods, EV-based percentage assessment is considered to be the best as it tends to be much less subjective.
Conditional Note/Associated Component: Shall use either activity duration percent complete or activity physical percent complete. Requires use of earned value technique.
Definition: An estimate, expressed as a percent, of the amount of work that has been completed on a schedule activity, measured in terms of either physical work progress or via the earning rules of earned value management.

Activity Remaining Duration	Required	Calculated/Manual

Data Format: Numeric
Behavior: Defines the length of time required to complete the activity as of the data date.
Good Practices: Once an activity begins but does not complete during a reporting cycle, a determination needs to be made as to the duration that remains to complete the work.
Conditional Note/Associated Component: Resource assignments may impact activity remaining duration.
Definition: The total number of work periods in calendar units, either equal to the original duration for an activity that has not started or between the data date of the project schedule and the CPM early finish date of a schedule activity that has an activity actual start date. This represents the time needed to complete a schedule activity where the work is in progress. Note: Prior to Actual Start, Activity Duration = Activity Remaining Duration

Activity Resource Actual Quantity   Required (RRC)   Manual / Calculated

Data Format: Numeric

Behavior: Measure of utilization of a resource at an activity level.

Good Practices: Resources should be identified and assigned. If resources are assigned, "activity actual resource quantity" needs to be used.

Conditional Note/Associated Component:

Definition: The unit to express the amount of a resource used for an activity since the activity actual start date.

Activity Resource Leveled Finish Date   Optional   Calculated

Data Format: Date

Behavior: Identifies the earliest finish for an activity based on resource limitations.

Good Practices: Resources should be identified and assigned. If resources are assigned and resource over allocations exists, resource leveling needs to be used.

Conditional Note/Associated Component:

Definition: The point in time associated with the activity scheduled finish date of a resource-limited schedule activity in a resource-limited schedule.

Activity Resource Leveled Start Date   Optional   Manual

Data Format: Date

Behavior: Defines the earliest start for an activity based on resource limitations.

Good Practices: Resources should be identified and assigned. If resources are assigned and there is an over allocation of resources, resource leveling should be used.

Conditional Note/Associated Component:

Definition: The point in time associated with the activity scheduled start date of a resource-limited schedule activity in a resource-limited schedule.

Activity Resource Total Quantity   Required (RRC)   Manual / Calculated

Data Format: Numeric

Behavior: Measure of resources required to accomplish an activity. The quantity is unique per resource per activity.

Good Practices: Resources should be identified and assigned. If resources are assigned, activity total resource quantity should be used.

Conditional Note/Associated Component: Cost

Definition: The unit to express resources required to complete the activity regardless of availability or assignment.

Activity Risk Criticality Index   Required (KRC)   Calculated

---

Data Format: Numeric

Behavior: The probability of an activity to become a member of a critical path.

Good Practices: A risk analysis process should be used for projects where stakeholders believe there is high risk. Risk analysis is appropriate for projects in which schedule variances have a significant impact on project objectives.

Conditional Note/Associated Component:

Definition: The probability that the schedule activity will be on a critical path, calculated by dividing the number of times the activity is on a critical path during simulation by the number of iterations in that simulation.

Activity Scope Definition   Optional   Manual

Data Format: Alphanumeric

Behavior: Allows user-defined information to be recorded about the work to be performed.

Good Practices: The activity scope definition should be provided for each activity to further bound the work.

Conditional Note/Associated Component:

Definition: Documented narrative describing the work represented by the activity.

Activity Total Duration   Required   Calculated/Manual

Data Format: Numeric

Behavior: Defines activity duration from start to finish.

Good Practices:

Conditional Note/Associated Component: Actual duration, remaining duration

Definition: The total number of work periods in calendar units to complete a schedule activity. For schedule activities in progress, it includes the activity actual duration plus the activity remaining duration.

Activity Work Percent Complete   Optional   Calculated/Manual

---

Data Format: Numeric (fractional)

Behavior: Represents the proportion of actual work effort completed at a given point in time.

Good Practices:

Conditional Note/Associated Component:

Definition: An estimate, expressed as a percent of the amount of work that has been completed on a schedule activity. It is usually based on the activity duration percent complete and the profile of work hours assigned to the activity.

As Late As Possible — Optional – Not scored — Manual

Data Format: Alphanumeric

Behavior: Allows an activity to be scheduled so that it finishes on its latest finish date given the present schedule model logic and constraints. The behavior of as late as possible constraints are scheduling tool dependent.

Good Practices: Constraints are not to be a replacement for schedule network logic. The "as late as possible constraint" should be used sparingly.

Conditional Note/Associated Component:

Definition: A constraint placed on an activity that will cause it to be scheduled to finish on a date without delaying successor activities.

As Soon As Possible — Optional – Not scored — Manual

Data Format: Alphanumeric

Behavior: Allows an activity to be scheduled so that it finishes on its CPM early finish date. The "as soon as possible constraint" is scheduling tool dependent.

Good Practices: Typically the default date constraint. Used for most activities in the schedule model.

Conditional Note/Associated Component: Project start date.

Definition: A constraint placed on an activity that will cause it to be scheduled to finish on the earliest date after the project start date based on any predecessor activities and schedule logic.

Baseline Schedule Model — Required

Data Format: Various

Behavior: Captures the scheduling components at the time the project plan was approved by the project stakeholders.

Good Practices:

Conditional Note/Associated Component: The development of the schedule model supports establishment and approval of an analysis point.

Definition: A baseline schedule model is a copy of the scheduling components at the time the project plan was approved by the project stakeholders (the latest approved schedule model) and is used for comparison to other schedule model instances.

Budget at Completion (BAC) — Required (ERC) — Calculated

Data Format: Number

Behavior: Defines the project authorized budget.

Good Practices: Include resources and associated costs in the schedule model to define the time-phased budget.

Conditional Note/Associated Component: A management-approved BAC may be called an approved baseline.

Definition: The sum total of resource costs listed in the schedule model that is approved by management. BAC may be calculated by activity and then summed to various levels.

Change Request Identifier   Optional   Manual

Data Format: Alphanumeric
Behavior: Identifies configuration controlled authorized changes to the schedule model.
Good Practices: As part of schedule configuration management, use the change request identifier to mark schedule model changes approved by configuration management processes. This item is normally addressed in a custom field.
Conditional Note/Associated Component: See the *Practice Standard for Configuration Management.*
Definition: The change request identifier is the primary key value for items in the program change log as related to the schedule model.

Control Account ID   Required (ERC)   Manual

Data Format: Alphanumeric
Behavior: Identifies tasks belonging to a stated cost collection account.
Good Practices: Include the Control Account Identifier when using earned value methodology in the schedule.
Conditional Note/Associated Component: See the *Practice Standard for Earned Value Management.*
Definition: An alphanumeric cost accounting identifier typically assigned at the intersection of the work breakdown structure and organizational breakdown structure at the level where costs will be collected. Control accounts contain work packages.

Control Account Manager (CAM)   Optional   Manual

Data Format: Alphanumeric
Behavior: Identifies the single person accountable for cost performance of a specific control account.
Good Practices: Include the CAM identifier when using earned value methodology in the schedule. Sometimes a reference number is used for a CAM without naming an individual.
Conditional Note/Associated Component: See the *Practice Standard for Earned Value Management.*
Definition: An alphanumeric designation of the single person accountable for the costs and achievement of the scope of work identified by the control account; this may be the name of an individual or a unique reference identifying the individual.

Cost Performance Index (CPI)   Optional   Calculated

Data Format: Number
Behavior: Defines cost performance relative to accomplishments and time-phased budget.
Good Practices: Include CPI when using earned value methodology in the schedule.
Conditional Note/Associated Component: See the *Practice Standard for Earned Value Management.*
Definition: EV/AC, calculated as time-phased values and used to measure the cost efficiency in a project. These values may be calculated at any schedule model outline level and between various data dates. If the calculation is performed using the project start date and the most current data date, the values are called "cumulative."

Cost Variance (CV)　　　　　　　　　　Optional　　　　　　　　Calculated

Data Format:　　Number
Behavior:　The time-phased deviation of achieved performance from actual costs.
Good Practices:　Include cost variance when using earned value methodology in the schedule.
Conditional Note/Associated Component:　See the *Practice Standard for Earned Value Management*.
Definition:　EV–AC, calculated as time-phased values and used to measure cost performance in a project. These values may be calculated at any schedule model outline level and between various data dates. If the calculation is performed using the project start date and the most current data date, the values are called "cumulative."

Cost Variance Percent (CV%)　　　　　Optional　　　　　　　　Calculated

Data Format:　　Number
Behavior:　The time-phased deviation of scheduled performance from actual achieved performance expressed as a percentage.
Good Practices:　Include cost variance percent when using earned value methodology in the schedule.
Conditional Note/Associated Component:　See the *Practice Standard for Earned Value Management*.
Definition:　$100 \times (EV - AC) / (EV)$, calculated as time-phased values. These values may be calculated at any schedule model outline level and between various data dates. If the calculation is performed using the project start date and the most current data date, the values are called "cumulative." When EV=0, CPI=0 regardless of AC.

Critical Path　　　　　　　　　　　　Required　　　　　　　　Calculated

Data Format:　　Alphanumeric (list of activities)
Behavior:　Identifies the activities on the critical path.
Good Practices:　To establish a meaningful critical path, it is necessary to develop logical and well-defined activity relationships with empirically derived durations for executing all the project activities in a practical manner. Therefore, there shall not be any open ends other than the project start and project finish. Constraints need to be restricted to only those that represent external or internal events that cannot be effectively addressed with activity logic.
Conditional Note/Associated Component:　Relationships defined for all activities.
Definition:　Generally, but not always, the sequence of schedule activities that determines the duration of the project. Generally, it is the longest path through the project. However, a critical path can end, as an example, on a schedule milestone that is in the middle of the schedule model and that has a finish-no-later-than imposed date schedule constraint. See also *project critical path*, *specified critical path*, and *critical path method*.

Custom Field　　　　　　　　　　　　Optional　　　　　　　　Manual

Data Format:　　Variable
Behavior:　Provides meta information about other schedule model data.
Good Practices:　The custom field can utilize any of the attribute types; alpha, alphanumeric, date, time, etc. A good practice is to use custom fields for sorting and grouping of activities in schedule model presentations.
Conditional Note/Associated Component:
Definition:　Data elements used as extended characteristic of schedule entities (e.g., code, field, tag, etc.).

Data Date	Required	Manual

Data Format: Date
Behavior: Defines the division between historical and future progress periods. Also known as status date.
Good Practices: The data date shall be advanced at the time of reporting status, at regular intervals.
Conditional Note/Associated Component:
Definition: The date (including time of day) through which the project status and progress were last determined and reported for analyses, such as scheduling and performance measurements. It is the last past historical date. Sometimes called as-of-date. (Scheduler caution: some project management software used for scheduling treats the data date as the future date immediately after status is reported.)

Driving Resources	Optional	Manual

Data Format: Flag (determined by algorithm (Boolean))
Behavior: Identifies a resource as driving to control the duration of activities.
Good Practices: Driving resources should be considered within the schedule.
Conditional Note/Associated Component:
Definition: Resources that are considered to have a direct impact on activity duration during resource leveling.

Earned Value (EV)	Required (ERC)	Calculated

Data Format: Number
Behavior: Measurement of accomplishment.
Good Practices: Include earned value when using earned value methodology in the schedule model.
Conditional Note/Associated Component: See the *Practice Standard for Earned Value Management*. This term is also known as budgeted cost of work performed (BCWP).
Definition: The time-phased value of the accomplished effort, independent of the cost needed to achieve the accomplishment; the cost that would be budgeted for the amount of completed work prior to its execution. When completed, EV = BAC. These values may be calculated at any schedule model outline level and between various data dates. If the calculation is performed using the project start date and the most current data date, the values are called "cumulative."

Earned Value Method	Optional	Manual

Data Format: Alphanumeric
Behavior: Identifies one of the recognized methods of collecting earned value as defined in the project's earned value management systems (EVMS).
Good Practices: For cost/schedule integration, include the earned value method when using earned value methodology in the schedule. The method stated in the schedule matches the earned value method stated in the work package.
Conditional Note/Associated Component: See the *Practice Standard for Earned Value Management*.
Definition: The alphanumeric designation of a specific method for collecting earned value in the schedule as defined in the EVMS.

Earned Value Weight | Optional | Manual

Data Format: Number

Behavior: Assigns a percentage of earned value (EV) for a work package to be allocated to specific activities.

Good Practices: When EV will be allocated on a percentage basis, use the EV weight in the schedule where appropriate.

Conditional Note/Associated Component: See the *Practice Standard for Earned Value Management.*

Definition: The percentage of EV allocated to a specific group of activities.

Estimate at Completion (EAC) | Required (ERC) | Calculated

Data Format: Number

Behavior: Defines the total cost, including actual costs already incurred, plus additional costs required to complete the effort.

Good Practices: Assign a value representing the projected total costs incurred upon completion, independent of an authorized budget.

Conditional Note/Associated Component:

Definition: AC + ETC, cumulative actual incurred costs (AC) plus anticipated costs to complete the remaining scope independent of budget. EAC is typically calculated for each activity and then summed to various levels. There are numerous methods to compute the value of additional costs estimated to complete the remaining scope.

Estimate to Complete (ETC) | Required (ERC) | Calculated

Data Format: Number

Behavior: Defines the cost required to complete the identified remaining scope, without regard to prior expenses or budget.

Good Practices: Assign a value representing the projected remaining cost to complete, independent of authorized budget.

Conditional Note/Associated Component:

Definition: Anticipated costs to complete the remaining scope independent of budget and prior actual costs. ETC is typically calculated for each activity and then summed to various levels. There are numerous methods to predict the value of remaining costs for the remaining scope.

Expected Finish   Optional – Not scored   Manual

Data Format: Date

Behavior: Imposes a finish date on an activity that determines the remaining duration of the activity after it has been reported as started with an actual start. The behavior of expected finish constraints are scheduling tool dependent.

Good Practices: Constraints are not to be a replacement for schedule network logic. The expected finish constraint should be used sparingly.

Conditional Note/Associated Component:

Definition: A date constraint placed on both the activity CPM early and late finish dates of an in-progress schedule activity that affects when the schedule activity can be scheduled for completion and is usually in the form of a fixed imposed date. This constraint requires the "activity remaining duration" to be set equal to the difference between the activity expected finish date and the data date to force the schedule activity to be scheduled to finish upon the imposed date.

Finish Not Earlier Than   Optional – Not scored   Manual

Data Format: Date

Behavior: Imposes a date on the finish of an activity prior to which the activity can not finish. The behavior of "finish not earlier than" is scheduling tool dependent.

Good Practices: Constraints are not to be a replacement for schedule network logic. The finish not earlier than constraint should be used sparingly.

Conditional Note/Associated Component:

Definition: A date constraint placed on the schedule activity that affects when a schedule activity can be scheduled and is usually in the form of a fixed imposed date. A finish not earlier than constraint prevents the activity from being scheduled to finish earlier than the imposed date. "Not earlier than" constraints impact only the CPM forward pass calculation and, therefore, only the CPM early dates of a schedule activity.

Finish Not Later Than   Optional   Manual

Data Format: Date

Behavior: Imposes a date on the finish of an activity specifying the latest date that an activity can finish. The behavior of "finish not later than" is scheduling tool dependent.

Good Practices: Constraints are not to be a replacement for schedule network logic. The "finish not later than" constraint should be used sparingly.

Conditional Note/Associated Component:

Definition: A date constraint placed on the schedule activity that affects when a schedule activity can be scheduled and is usually in the form of a fixed imposed date. A finish not later than constraint prevents the activity from being scheduled to finish later than the imposed date. "Not later than" constraints impact only the CPM backward pass calculation and, therefore, the CPM calculated late dates of a schedule activity.

Finish On   Optional – Not scored   Manual

Data Format: Date

Behavior: Imposes a date on the finish of an activity on which it shall finish. Impacts both the CPM forward and the CPM backward pass calculation and, therefore, both CPM early and late dates. This causes the activity to have a zero total float while its predecessors and successors may have different float values. The finish on date will move with the data date if the data date is later than the finish on date and if the activity is not complete. The behavior of finish on constraints are scheduling tool dependent.

Good Practices: Constraints are not to be a replacement for schedule network logic. Since this constraint overrides the CPM calculation, this component should not be used.

Conditional Note/Associated Component:

Definition: A date constraint placed on the schedule activity that requires the schedule activity to finish on a specific date. Schedule calculations do not override this constraint. Therefore an imposed "finish on" sets the CPM forward pass early dates for all paths leading from and the CPM late dates on paths leading to the activity. This is also known as Must Finish On.

Finish to Finish   Optional   Manual

Data Format: Alphanumeric (activity ID)

Behavior: Specifies for two activities that the successor activity cannot be completed until the predecessor activity is completed.

Good Practices: All activities, except the first and last activities, shall have at least one "?S" predecessor relationship and one "F?" successor relationship, where "?" can be either an S or F, regardless of any other relationships that may be present. (Where S = start and F = finish).

Conditional Note/Associated Component:

Definition: The logical relationship where completion of work of the successor activity cannot finish until the completion of work of the predecessor activity.

Finish to Start   Required   Manual

Data Format: Alphanumeric (activity ID)

Behavior: Specifies for two activities that the successor activity cannot be started until the predecessor activity is completed.

Good Practices: All activities, except the first and last activity, shall have at least one "?S" predecessor relationship and one "F?" successor relationship, where "?" can be either an S or F, regardless of any other relationships that may be present. (Where S = start and F = finish. Typically the most commonly used relationship.

Conditional Note/Associated Component:

Definition: The logical relationship where initiation of work of the successor activity depends upon the completion of work of the predecessor activity.

Free Float	Required	Calculated

Data Format: Numeric

Behavior: Represents the amount of time an activity can delay its early finish without impacting successor activities early start. It is the difference between an activity's early finish date and the earliest start date of the closest of its successors. As progress is recorded, this value may change. This value may also change if remaining work, logic, or durations are revised.

Good Practices: Free float may be used to provide an early indication of activity or schedule slippage.

Conditional Note/Associated Component:

Definition: The amount of time that a schedule activity can be delayed without delaying the CPM early start of immediately following schedule activities. See also *total float.*

Lag	Optional	Manual

Data Format: Numeric

Behavior: Modifies a logical relationship to impose a delay in the start or finish of the successor activity.

Good Practices: Lags are not to be a replacement for schedule network logic or activities. Lags should be used sparingly. Lags should only be used for an unchanging period of time that occurs between one activity and another. A lag should not take resources.

Conditional Note/Associated Component:

Definition: A modification of a logical relationship that directs a delay in the successor activity. For example, in a finish-to-start dependency with a 10-day lag, the successor activity cannot start until 10 days after the predecessor activity has finished. See also *lead.*

Lead	Optional – Not scored	Manual

Data Format: Numeric

Behavior: Modifies a logical relationship to impose an acceleration in the start or finish of the successor activity, analogous to "negative" lag.

Good Practices: Leads are not a replacement for schedule network logic or activities. Leads should be used rarely. Leads will only be used for an unchanging period of time that occurs between one activity and another. A lead should not take resources.

Conditional Note/Associated Component:

Definition: A modification of a logical relationship that allows an acceleration of the successor activity. For example, in a finish-to-start dependency with a 10-day lead, the successor activity can start 10 days before the predecessor activity has finished. A negative lead is equivalent to a positive lag. See also *lag.*

Mandatory Finish Date	Optional – Not scored	Manual

Data Format: Date

Behavior: Imposes a date on the finish of an activity on which it shall finish. Impacts both the CPM forward and the backward pass date calculations and hence both early and late dates. This causes the activity to have a zero total float while its predecessors and successors may have different float values. The behavior of mandatory finish date constraints are scheduling tool dependent.

Good Practices: Constraints are not to be a replacement for schedule network logic. Since this constraint overrides the CPM calculation, this component should not be used.

Conditional Note/Associated Component:

Definition: A date constraint placed on the schedule activity that requires the schedule activity to finish on a specific date. Schedule calculations do not override this constraint. Therefore an imposed mandatory finish sets the CPM early finish dates for all paths leading from and the late finish dates on paths leading to the activity. Also known as Must Finish On.

Mandatory Start Date	Optional – Not scored	Manual

Data Format: Date

Behavior: Imposes a date on the start of an activity on which it shall start. Impacts both the CPM forward and the backward pass calculations and, hence, both CPM early and late dates. This causes the activity to have a zero total float while its predecessors and successors may have different float values. The behavior of mandatory start date constraints are scheduling tool dependent.

Good Practices: Constraints are not to be a replacement for schedule network logic. Since this constraint overrides the CPM calculation, this component should not be used.

Conditional Note/Associated Component:

Definition: A date constraint placed on the schedule activity that requires the schedule activity to start on a specific date. Schedule calculations do not override this constraint. Therefore, an imposed mandatory start sets the CPM early dates for all paths leading from and the CPM late dates on paths leading to the activity. Also known as Must Start On.

Milestone	Required	Calculated

Data Format: Flag (determined by algorithm (Boolean))

Behavior: An activity that identifies a significant event.

Good Practices: The milestone has no resources assigned and no duration. At a minimum a project start and finish milestone needs to be present in the schedule. Milestone indicator should have a unique shape such as a diamond.

Conditional Note/Associated Component:

Definition: A significant point or event in the project. See also *schedule milestone*.

Planned Value (PV)	Required (ERC)	Calculated

Data Format: Number

Behavior: The time-phased measurement of anticipated expenditures.

Good Practices: Include planned value when using earned value methodology in the schedule model.

Conditional Note/Associated Component: See the *Practice Standard for Earned Value Management*. This term is also known as budgeted cost of work scheduled (BCWS). PV is sometimes known as baseline plan.

Definition: The time-phased value of the management approved intended and necessary expenditures to achieve the defined scope. When the scope is completed, PV = BAC. These values may be calculated at any schedule model outline level and between various data dates. If the calculation is performed using the project start date and the most current data date, the values are called "cumulative."

Probability Risk Distribution	Required (KRC)	Calculated

Data Format: Numeric

Behavior: Probability risk distributions should be assigned to activities for quantitative risk analysis. Common probability risk distributions include: normal—or bell curve, log normal, uniform, triangular, Beta, and discrete (user-defined).

Good Practices: May be found in the *Practice Standard for Project Risk Management*. Probability risk distribution should be assigned to each activity in the schedule model. Data, usually judgmentally determined, is collected from project participants and other experts during risk interviews or workshops.

Conditional Note/Associated Component:

Definition: Defines the probability that particular attributes or ranges of attributes will be or have been observed.

Project Actual Duration	Required	Calculated

Data Format: Numeric

Behavior: Identifies the length of time that has elapsed since the project plan began.

Good Practices:

Conditional Note/Associated Component:

Definition: The total number of work periods in calendar units between the project actual start date of the project and either the data date of the schedule model instance if the project is in progress or the project actual finish date if the project is complete.

Project Actual Finish Date	Required	Calculated

Data Format: Date

Behavior: Identifies the actual finish of the project based on the last activity actual finish date.

Good Practices:

Conditional Note/Associated Component:

Definition: The point in time associated with the "activity actual finish date" of the last schedule activity in the project.

Project Actual Start Date   Required   Calculated

Data Format: Date
Behavior: Defines the actual start of the project's earliest activity.
Good Practices:
Conditional Note/Associated Component: From detail.
Definition: The point in time associated with the "activity actual start date" of the earliest schedule activity in the project.

Project Calendar   Required   Manual

Data Format: Date/Time
Behavior: Defines the default working periods for the project
Good Practices: At the project level, this will constitute the primary or default calendar for the project.
Conditional Note/Associated Component:
Definition: A calendar of working and non-working periods that establish when schedule activities are worked and when schedule activities are idle. Typically defines holidays, weekends, and shift hours. The calendar initially assigned to schedule activities and resources. See also *activity calendar* and *resource calendar*.

Project Cost Category   Optional   Manual

Data Format: Alphanumeric
Behavior: Provides additional breakdowns that can be assigned for a specific cost account within the project.
Good Practices: For accounting purposes, costs should be broken down into such categories as direct, indirect, labor, material, equipment, etc.
Conditional Note/Associated Component:
Definition: Accounting elements used to integrate traditional chart of account line items with the project cost accounting structure.

Project Description   Optional   Manual

Data Format: Alphanumeric
Behavior: Describes with a short phrase, the project.
Good Practices: The project description should summarize the scope of work for the entire project.
Conditional Note/Associated Component:
Definition: Documented narrative summary of the project scope statement.

Project Duration Percent Complete	Required (see Project Physical Percent Complete)	Calculated

Data Format: Numeric (fractional)

Behavior: Represents the progress of the project as a percentage of total expected project duration.

Good Practices:

Conditional Note/Associated Component: Shall use either project duration percent complete or project physical percent complete.

Definition: An estimate, expressed as a percentage, of the entire project duration that has been completed on the project.

Project Early Finish Date	Required	Calculated

Data Format: Date

Behavior: Identifies the early finish of last activity.

Good Practices: Derived from the CPM calculations.

Conditional Note/Associated Component:

Definition: The point in time associated with the activity early finish date of the last schedule activity of the project.

Project Early Start Date	Required	Calculated

Data Format: Date

Behavior: Defines the CPM early start of the project's first activity, based on the CPM forward pass.

Good Practices: Derived from the CPM calculations.

Conditional Note/Associated Component:

Definition: The earliest possible point in time associated with the beginning of the first schedule activity of the project.

Project Finish Constraint	Optional	Manual

Data Format: Date

Behavior: Provides the starting point for the CPM backward pass for the project. The constraint is used as the starting point for the backward pass calculation for any activities in the schedule model with no successors and no CPM backward pass constraints. This date may be earlier or later than the project finish date that is calculated from the CPM forward pass.

Good Practices: The finish date, typically defined by the customer, and included in the schedule model. Effort needs to be made to develop an achievable schedule model with non-negative total float. This effort should result in a schedule model with a level of risk acceptable to all stakeholders. If this is not accomplished, the stakeholder defining the project finish constraint shall be informed and a mitigation plan agreed upon.

Conditional Note/Associated Component:

Definition: A limitation or restraint placed on the project late finish date that affects when the project needs to finish and is usually in the form of a fixed imposed date.

Project Late Finish Date	Required	Calculated

Data Format: Date
Behavior: Identifies the late finish of last activity.
Good Practices: Derived from the CPM calculations.
Conditional Note/Associated Component:
Definition: The point in time associated with the activity late finish date of the last schedule activity of the project.

Project Late Start Date	Required	Calculated

Data Format: Date
Behavior: Defines the late start of the project's first activity, based on the backward pass.
Good Practices: Derived from the CPM calculations.
Conditional Note/Associated Component:
Definition: The latest possible point in time associated with the beginning of the first schedule activity of the project.

Project Manager	Optional	Manual

Data Format: Alphanumeric
Behavior: Shows the name of the project manager.
Good Practices: Should be displayed on all output.
Conditional Note/Associated Component:
Definition: The person assigned by the performing organization to achieve the project objectives.

Project Name	Required	Manual

Data Format: Alphanumeric
Behavior: Describes, in a short form, the project.
Good Practices:
Conditional Note/Associated Component:
Definition: A short phrase or label for each project, used in conjunction with the project identifier to differentiate a particular project from other projects in a program. Also known as project title.

Project Physical Percent Complete	Required (see Project Duration Percent Complete)	Calculated

Data Format: Numeric (fractional)

Behavior: Represents the progress of the project as a percentage of total physical work to be done. At the project level, this value is typically calculated, using earned value management techniques. As progress is recorded, the earned value at the activity level is calculated.

Good Practices: Performed in accordance with *Practice Standard for Earned Value Management*. Project physical percent complete is determined by dividing the summarized earned value units by the project budget in the same units.

Conditional Note/Associated Component: Requires use of earned value technique. Shall use either project duration percent complete or project physical percent complete.

Definition: A calculation, expressed as a percent, of the amount of work that has been completed on the project, measured in terms of physical work progress.

Project Remaining Duration	Required	Calculated

Data Format: Numeric

Behavior: Identifies the length of time required to complete the project from the data date.

Good Practices: Once a project begins but does not complete during a reporting cycle, a determination is made as to the duration that remains to complete the work.

Conditional Note/Associated Component:

Definition: The total number of work periods in calendar units, either equal to the original duration for a project that has not started or between the data date of the schedule model and the project early finish date of a project that has at least one activity actual start date. This represents the time needed to complete a project where the work is in progress.

Project Resource Actual Quantity	Required (RRC)	Manual / Calculated

Data Format: Numeric

Behavior: Measure of resources utilization for the project as of data date.

Good Practices: Resources should be identified and assigned. If resources are assigned, project actual quantity should be used.

Conditional Note/Associated Component:

Definition: The unit to express resources utilization for the project as of data date.

Project Resource Leveled Finish Date	Optional	Calculated

Data Format: Date

Behavior: Identifies the earliest finish for a project based on resource limitations.

Good Practices: Resources should be identified and assigned. If resources are assigned and resource over allocations exist, resource leveling should be used.

Conditional Note/Associated Component:

Definition: The point in time associated with the last activity scheduled finish date of a resource-limited schedule activity in a resource-limited schedule.

Project Resource Leveled Start Date   Optional   Calculated

Data Format: Dates
Behavior: Identifies the earliest activity start date as constrained by the resource availability.
Good Practices: Resources should be identified and assigned. If an assigned resource is limited, resource leveling should be performed.
Conditional Note/Associated Component:
Definition: The start date of a project based on the consideration of resource availabilities, limitations, and quantities.

Project Resource Total Quantity   Required (RRC)   Manual / Calculated

Data Format: Numeric
Behavior: Measure of the project's resource assignments, usually expressed as resource type or measure.
Good Practices: Resources should be identified and assigned. If resources are assigned, project total quantity should be used.
Conditional Note/Associated Component:
Definition: The unit to express resource assignments across all activities of the project.

Project Start Constraint   Optional   Manual

Data Format: Date
Behavior: Provides the starting point for the forward pass for the project. Will be used to as the starting point for the forward pass calculation for any activities in the schedule model with no predecessors and no forward pass constraints.
Good Practices: The start date is typically defined by the customer and included in the schedule model. Effort needs to be made to develop an achievable schedule model that meets the project start constraint. This effort should account for available resources and result in a schedule model with a level of risk acceptable to all stakeholders. If this is not accomplished, the stakeholder defining the project start constraint shall be informed and a mitigation plan agreed upon.
Conditional Note/Associated Component:
Definition: A limitation or restraint placed on the project early start date that affects when the project can start and is usually in the form of a fixed imposed date.

Project Total Duration   Required   Calculated

Data Format: Numeric
Behavior: Identifies the duration of the project from start to finish
Good Practices:
Conditional Note/Associated Component:
Definition: The total number of work periods in calendar units to complete a project. For a project in progress, it includes the project actual duration plus the project remaining duration.

Resource Assignment   Required (RRC)   Manual

Data Format: Numeric
Behavior: Action to assign a resource to an activity.
Good Practices: Resources should be identified and assigned. If resources are assigned, resource assignment will be used.
Conditional Note/Associated Component:
Definition: The activity of allocating a resource to a specific schedule model element.

Resource Availability   Required (RRC)   Manual

Data Format: Alphanumeric
Behavior: Establishes availability of a resource to support the project.
Good Practices: This value does not reflect the current and project resource assignments for the indicated resource.
Conditional Note/Associated Component:
Definition: The dates and number of work periods in calendar units that a given resource can be utilized according to the appropriate resource calendar.

Resource Calendar   Required (RRC)   Manual

Data Format: Date/Time
Behavior: Defines the working periods for the resource.
Good Practices:
Conditional Note/Associated Component:
Definition: A calendar of working and non-working periods assigned to the resource which defines the work periods and non-work periods in calendar format. Typically defines resource specific holidays and resource availability periods. See also *project calendar* and *activity calendar*.

Resource Description   Required (RRC)   Manual

Data Format: Alphanumeric
Behavior: Describes with a short phrase the resource and its associated domain.
Good Practices: Resources should be identified and assigned. If a resource is identified, the resource description is needed. All resource descriptions shall be unique.
Conditional Note/Associated Component:
Definition: A phrase that identifies a resource by type, role, or individual. Also known as Resource Name.

Resource ID   Required (RRC)   Calculated

Data Format: Alphanumeric
Behavior: Identifies the assigned resource.
Good Practices: Resources should be identified and assigned. If a resource is identified, the resource ID needs to be used. All resource IDs shall be unique.
Conditional Note/Associated Component:
Definition: A short unique numeric or text description assigned to each specific resource to differentiate that resource from other resources. The resource ID is typically unique within any one project.

Resource Lag	Optional	Manual

Data Format: Numeric

Behavior: Defines the time from the start of the activity that a specific resource may begin work.

Good Practices: Resources should be identified and assigned. Resource lags are only to be used for an unchanging period of time that should occur between the start of the activity and the use of the resource.

Conditional Note/Associated Component:

Definition: The number of calendar units a resource is to wait after the activity start date before beginning work on the schedule activity.

Resource Leveling	Optional	Calculated

Data Format: Formula

Behavior: Involves the process of recalculating the scheduled dates, based on the availability of resources.

Good Practices: Resource leveling requires the assignment of resource limits or availabilities, as well as some prioritizing criteria to resolve resource conflicts. The most often used prioritizing criterion is total float. Often this leveling effort also includes financial considerations as well as the limits on physical resources of any kind. Calculated results should be manually evaluated against expectations and historical references.

Conditional Note/Associated Component:

Definition: Any form of schedule network analysis in which scheduling decisions (start and finish dates) are driven by resource constraints (e.g., limited resource availability or difficult-to-manage changes in resource availability levels).

Resource Library/Dictionary	Required (RRC)	Manual

Data Format: Alphanumeric

Behavior: Provides a listing of resources applied to activities in the schedule model.

Good Practices: Resources should be identified and assigned. A resource library or dictionary should be organized into a meaningful structure.

Conditional Note/Associated Component:

Definition: A documented tabulation containing the complete list, including resource attributes, of all resources that can be assigned to project activities. Also known as a resource dictionary.

Resource Rates/Prices	Optional	Manual

Data Format: Numeric

Behavior: Defines the cost per time unit for a specific resource.

Good Practices: Resources should be identified and assigned. If resources are assigned, resource rates/prices should be used.

Conditional Note/Associated Component:

Definition: The unit cost rate assigned to a specific resource, including known rate escalations.

Resource Type	Required (RRC)	Manual

Data Format: Alphanumeric

Behavior: Indicates the classification of the resource.

Good Practices: Resources should be identified and assigned. If a resource is identified, the resource type should be used.

Conditional Note/Associated Component:

Definition: A unique designation that differentiates a resource by skills, capabilities, or other attributes. An individual resource has one resource type and many resources may have the same resource type.

Risk ID	Required (KRC)	Manual / Calculated

Data Format: Alphanumeric

Behavior: Distinguishes risks on the project's risk register.

Good Practices: May be found in the *Practice Standard for Project Risk Management.* Risk IDs are mapped to activities in the schedule model where appropriate.

Conditional Note/Associated Component:

Definition: A short unique numeric or text identification assigned to each risk on the project's risk register.

Schedule Model ID	Required	Manual

Data Format: Alphanumeric

Behavior: Identifies the scheduled project.

Good Practices: Shall be a unique identifier that can be automatically generated or follows a numbering scheme appropriate for the enterprise. It is helpful to assign a reasoned structure or "coding" to the schedule model ID.

Conditional Note/Associated Component:

Definition: A short unique numeric or text identification assigned to each schedule model to differentiate that schedule model from others. Also known as the project identifier.

Schedule Model Level	Optional	Manual

Data Format: Numeric

Behavior: Defines the granularity or levels of detail of the schedule or its presentation.

Good Practices: Regardless of the physical level depth of the overall schedule, it is recommended that the following schedule level definitions be used:

1. *Level 1—Executive Summary.* This is a summary level schedule, usually only one page that will include the major contractual milestones and summary level activities.
2. *Level 2—Management Summary.* This is a more extensive summary level schedule, usually four to five pages that will include the Level 1 and report on similar activities by area or capital equipment.
3. *Level 3—Publication Schedule.* This will be the level of detail used to support the monthly report. It will include all major milestones, major elements of engineering, procurement, construction, and start-up.
4. *Level 4—Execution Planning.* This supports the construction and commissioning teams in their overall planning of the project. All activities of over a week's duration should normally be shown. The 3-week look-ahead schedule is produced from Level 4 and above.
5. *Level 5—Detailed Planning.* This level of detail will support the short-term planning for the field, normally for those activities of less than 1-week duration. Workarounds and critical areas can be exploded here.

Conditional Note/Associated Component:

Definition: A project team specified rule for the relative granularity of schedule activities in the overall schedule model.

Schedule Model Presentation	Required	Manual

Data Format: Graphical

Behavior: Displays schedule data.

Good Practices:
1. A visual display of the schedule model activities should be employed as a bar chart.
2. Outputs shall depict the date upon which the output is generated.
3. Descriptions of the output and major items within the output shall be included.
4. Outputs should show both progress and the current data date.
5. Any project network diagram should have as few logic crossover points as possible, while ensuring sufficient space to represent relationship lines. (See Figure 2-3 for example.)

Conditional Note/Associated Component:

Definition: An output from schedule model instances, used to communicate project specific data for reporting, analysis, and decision making

Schedule Model Version | Required | Calculated

Data Format: Alphanumeric
Behavior: Indicates which revision of the model the schedule represents.
Good Practices: The version number should be incremented in a consistent manner as successive changes are made, resulting in different versions of the schedule.
Conditional Note/Associated Component:
Definition: A designation of the instance of a schedule model. Examples include as-of date, revision number, and agreed versioning codes, among others.

Schedule Performance Index (SPI) | Optional | Calculated

Data Format: Number
Behavior: Defines schedule performance comparing accomplished work to scheduled work.
Good Practices: Include SPI when using earned value methodology in the schedule.
Conditional Note/Associated Component: See the *Practice Standard for Earned Value Management*.
Definition: EV/PV, calculated as time-phased values and used to measure a progress relative to the schedule. These values may be calculated at any schedule model outline level and between various data dates. If the calculation is performed using the project start date and the most current data date, the values are called "cumulative."

Schedule Variance (SV) | Optional | Calculated

Data Format: Number
Behavior: Deviation of scheduled performance from actual achieved performance.
Good Practices: Include schedule variance when using earned value methodology in the schedule.
Conditional Note/Associated Component: See the *Practice Standard for Earned Value Management*.
Definition: EV–PV, calculated as time-phased values and used to measure a progress relative to the schedule. These values may be calculated at any schedule model outline level and between various data dates. If the calculation is performed using the project start date and the most current data date, the values are called "cumulative."

Schedule Variance Percent (SV%) | Optional | Calculated

Data Format: Number
Behavior: Deviation of scheduled performance from actual achieved performance.
Good Practices: Include schedule variance percent when using earned value methodology in the schedule.
Conditional Note/Associated Component: See the *Practice Standard for Earned Value Management*.
Definition: $100 \times (EV–PV) / (PV)$, calculated as time-phased values. These values may be calculated at any schedule model outline level and between various data dates. If the calculation is performed using the project start date and the most current data date, the values are called "cumulative."

Start Not Earlier Than   Optional – Not scored   Manual

Data Format: Date

Behavior: Imposes a date on the start of an activity prior to which the activity can not start. "Not earlier than" constraints impact only the forward pass calculation and hence the early dates of an activity.

Good Practices: Constraints are not to be a replacement for schedule network logic. The "start not earlier than" constraint should be used sparingly.

Conditional Note/Associated Component:

Definition: A date constraint placed on the schedule activity that affects when a schedule activity can be scheduled and is usually in the form of a fixed imposed date. A "start not earlier" than constraint prevents the schedule activity from being scheduled to start earlier than the imposed date.

Start Not Later Than   Optional – Not scored   Manual

Data Format: Date

Behavior: Imposes a date on the start of an activity specifying the latest date that an activity can start.

Good Practices: Constraints are not to be a replacement for schedule network logic. The start not later than constraint should be used sparingly.

Conditional Note/Associated Component:

Definition: A date constraint placed on the schedule activity that affects when a schedule activity can be scheduled and is usually in the form of a fixed imposed date. A "start not later than" constraint prevents the schedule activity from being scheduled to start later than the imposed date.

Start On   Optional – Not scored   Manual

Data Format: Date

Behavior: Imposes a date on the start of an activity on which it shall start. Impacts both the forward and the backward pass calculations and, therefore, both early and late dates. This causes the activity to have a zero total float while its predecessors and successors may have different float values. The start on date will move with the data date if the data date is later than the start on date. The behavior of start on constraints are scheduling tool dependent.

Good Practices: Constraints are not to be a replacement for schedule network logic. Since this constraint overrides the CPM calculation, this component should not be used.

Conditional Note/Associated Component:

Definition: A date constraint placed on the schedule activity that requires the schedule activity to start on a specific date. Schedule calculations do not override this constraint. Therefore, an imposed "start on" sets the early dates for all paths leading from and the late dates on paths leading to the activity.

Start to Finish	Optional – Not scored	Manual

Data Format: Alphanumeric (Activity ID)

Behavior: Specifies for two activities that the successor activity cannot be finished until the predecessor activity is started.

Good Practices: All activities, except the first and last activity, shall have at least one "?S" predecessor relationship and one "F?" successor relationship, where "?" can be either an S or F, regardless of any other relationships that may be present (where S = start and F = finish).

Conditional Note/Associated Component:

Definition: The logical relationship where completion of the successor schedule activity is dependent upon the initiation of the predecessor schedule activity. See also *logical relationship*.

Start to Start	Optional	Manual

Data Format: Alphanumeric (Activity ID)

Behavior: Specifies for two activities that the successor activity cannot be started until the predecessor activity is started.

Good Practices: All activities, except the first and last activity, shall have at least one "?S" predecessor relationship and one "F?" successor relationship, where "?"can be either an S or F, regardless of any other relationships that may be present (where S = start and F = finish).

Conditional Note/Associated Component:

Definition: The logical relationship where initiation of the work of the successor schedule activity depends upon the initiation of the work of the predecessor schedule activity. See also *logical relationship*.

Summary Activity	Optional	Calculated

Data Format: Alphanumeric

Behavior: Inherits information from subordinate activities. May be expressed as a roll-up activity or hammock.

Good Practices: Used for vertical traceability and roll-up.

Conditional Note/Associated Component:

Definition: A group of related schedule activities aggregated at some summary level, and displayed/reported as a single activity at that summary level. See also *subnetwork, subproject*.

Target Schedule Model	Optional	

Data Format: Various

Behavior: Captures the scheduling components for a target schedule model.

Good Practices:

Conditional Note/Associated Component:

Definition: A target schedule model is a copy of the scheduling components used for comparison to other schedule models. A target schedule model may be created from any version of the schedule model, for example, last update period.

To Complete Performance Index (TCPI)   Optional   Calculated

Data Format: Number
Behavior: Measure of cost performance required to finish the project at the stated EAC or the stated BAC.
Good Practices: Include TCPI when using earned value methodology in the schedule.
Conditional Note/Associated Component: See the *Practice Standard for Earned Value Management.*
Definition: TCPI is remaining effort divided by remaining budget (or authorized remaining funds).

$$TCPI_{BAC} = \frac{(BAC - EV_{CUM})}{(BAC - AC_{CUM})}$$

$$TCPI_{EAC} = \frac{(BAC - EV_{CUM})}{(EAC - AC_{CUM})}$$

Total Float   Required   Calculated

Data Format: Numeric
Behavior: Represents the amount of time an activity can delay its CPM early start or CPM early finish without impacting the CPM late finish of the project or violating a schedule constraint. It is computed as the difference between the CPM late and early dates of the activity, calculated from the CPM backward and forward passes respectively. As progress is recorded, this value may change. This value may also change if remaining work logic or durations are revised.
Good Practices: Total float may be used to provide an early indication of potential project completion slippage. This is done by constraining the project finish milestone with a finish on constraint.
Conditional Note/Associated Component:
Definition: The total amount of time that a schedule activity may be delayed from its activity CPM early start date or activity CPM early finish date without delaying the project CPM late finish date or violating a schedule constraint. Calculated using the critical path method technique and by subtracting the activity CPM early finish date from the activity CPM late finish date or subtracting the activity CPM early start date from the activity CPM late start date, with that difference expressed in calendar units. A total float value less than zero indicates that the activity CPM late date is scheduled prior to the activity CPM early date and the path that includes the activity cannot be completed in time to meet the CPM late finish of the project. A total float value of zero or greater indicates that the path that includes the activity can be completed in time to meet the CPM late finish of the project and some schedule activities on that path may be able to be delayed. See also *free float.*

Unit of Measure   Required   Manual

Data Format: Alphanumeric
Behavior: Provides quantifiable units for various components across the schedule.
Good Practices: Units of measure should be defined consistently throughout the schedule.
Conditional Note/Associated Component:
Definition: A designation of the type of quantity being measured, such as work-hours, cubic yards, or lines of code.

Variance	Optional	Calculated

Data Format: Numeric

Behavior: Quantifies departure from a date reference point (such as start date, finish date, cost, baseline dates and cost, and duration).

Good Practices: The variance should be reviewed for trends at regular intervals to give early indications of deviation and to determine if corrective action is required.

Conditional Note/Associated Component:

Definition: The difference between two selected attributes expressed in appropriate units such as work days, or currency.

WBS ID	Required (ERC)	Manual

Data Format: Alphanumeric

Behavior: Maps the activity or task to the work breakdown structure of the project. Defines the "parent element" of the activity within the WBS.

Good Practices: May be found in the *Practice Standard for Work Breakdown Structures.*

Conditional Note/Associated Component:

Definition: A short unique numeric or text identification assigned to each work breakdown structure (WBS) element to differentiate a particular WBS from any other WBS element in a program.

Work Package Identifier	Required (ERC)	Manual

Behavior: Identifies the EVMS work package in the schedules.

Good Practices: For cost/schedule integration, include the work package identifier when using earned value methodology in the schedule. A work package may contain multiple WBS elements. The work package identifier for an activity will contain a single value that maps it to a single work package.

Conditional Note/Associated Component: See the *Practice Standard for Earned Value Management* and the *Practice Standard for Work Breakdown Structure.*

Definition: The work package identifier is an alphanumeric designation of a specific work package in the EVMS.

CHAPTER 5

CONFORMANCE INDEX

This chapter is designed to provide an overview of the Conformance Index process. This chapter is divided into the following sections:

5.1 Conformance Overview

5.1.1 Categories of components

5.1.2 Utilization of components

5.1.3 Conformance assessment

5.2 Conformance Assessment Process

Each section provides additional dialogue on this practice standard's content and terminology.

5.1 Conformance Overview

The conformance index provides a means to assess how well a specific schedule model incorporates the guidelines, definitions, behaviors and good practices for the components as defined in this *Practice Standard for Scheduling* (Chapter 4). While some project managers may choose not to include some of these core required components (CRC), in doing so, the resulting schedule model is not in conformance with this practice standard and may not be viable. The basic premise is that as the conformance index increases, so does the proper application of the schedule model components and the likelihood that the developed schedule model represents a sound plan. The index was also constructed to reflect where the weaknesses of the developed schedule model exist and the areas most in need of improvement. Scheduling concepts, behaviors, attributes, and good practices are defined for all of the schedule model components. Schedule model conformance is assessed by evaluating the existence and proper utilization of the various components defined in this practice standard in accordance with the good practices.

5.1.1 Categories of Components

The component list in Chapter 4 identifies those components that are:

- "required" in a schedule model

- "optional" components that may be present but are not required

- "not scored (NS)" components, which are optional components that may be present in a schedule model but are not scored in the conformance index

---

The required core components can be defined by four different groups as listed below:

- The core components are required regardless of project complexity and are known as the core required components (CRC).

- The resource required components (RRC) are required if the project documents require resource loading.

- The earned value management components (ERC) are required if the project documents require EVM to be utilized on the project.

- The risk required components (KRC) are required if the project documents require risk concepts to be considered during the schedule development and maintenance.

5.1.2 Utilization of Schedule Components

The use of schedule components in a given schedule model is usually driven by the size of the project, the complexity of the project, or the experience of the scheduler or management team. Core components (CRC) are always required on any schedule regardless of the project-defined requirements in order to be in conformance with this practice standard. The other types of required components are applied for a specific project dependent on that project's requirements. These requirements are defined by various project documents and are typically contained within the organizational process assets, the project contract language, or the schedule model management plan for the project, but can also be any other written document.

The RRC, ERC and KRC are conditionally based on project requirements. For example, if the project requires that resources be loaded on the project and there are no other requirements for earned value management or risk management, then the total required components are CRC + RRC. In a similar manner, each required area will be added to the CRC when they are required by the project. If resources, risk, and EVM are required, then the required components are CRC + RRC + ERC + KRC. As the complexity of the requirements on the project increases, so does the number of total required components.

The required components need to be fully utilized in order to achieve a minimum acceptable level of conformance. If the project documents do not provide requirements for the schedule, then only the CRC components are required, and the RRC, ERC, and KRC remain optional components for that project. Scoring for the conformance index is done in accordance with Appendix D which divides the components into three basic categories: core required components (CRC), conditionally required components (RRC, ERC, KRC), and optional components.

The conformance index process provides a means of adjusting the index value when optional components are utilized. Existence of a component, in and of itself, is not sufficient to add to the score. Use of optional components can add to the index only if these components are in full accord with the good practice recommendations defined in the components list in Chapter 4. The NS components can be present in a schedule model but are not counted in the conformance index per the component list in Chapter 4.

5.1.3 Conformance Assessment

The assessment process is comprised of two parts: one for the application of required components and one assessment for the application of optional components. These two parts are added together to obtain a total index value. The resulting scores from these two assessments are added together to obtain a total index value. The assessment process is explained in greater detail in Section 5.2. The critical concept is that the required components have to be present before a conformance index value can be recorded; the specific required components can change based on project requirements. The CRC shall always be present regardless of the project scope complexity.

Once the schedule model has been assessed for incorporation of the appropriate required components, greater degrees of conformance can be achieved through the proper utilization of the available optional schedule components. Optional components can only be counted if they properly and completely adhere to the definitions, behaviors, and good practices defined in Chapter 4. Optional components should only be used to support the needs of a specific project—never just to increase the index value. As a general rule, the use of optional components would be expected to be found in more sophisticated organizations or more complex schedule models. Schedule models that do not fully utilize all of the required components and their concepts are considered developmental in nature. Developmental schedule models may still be assessed with a conformance index value but reflected as "does not meet minimum conformance standards."

The schedule model conformance assessment process is designed to support a manual assessment. When a component is present in the schedule model and properly utilized, one point is earned. The ratio of the total number of points (required plus optional) earned in relation to the total possible number of points that could be awarded represents the conformance value and is expressed as a percentage on the continuum from 0 to 100. The exception to this rule involves the required components. As stated previously, if the required components, as defined by the project requirements, are not fully utilized (100% employed), then the schedule model does not meet minimum conformance with this practice standard. If this minimum threshold is achieved, then the ratio value is depicted on the continuum or sliding scale, with (35) being the lowest and (100) being the highest (See Table 5-1). The lowest value (35) represents the ratio which would come from only the required components (CCR), all of which are necessary in every schedule model.

If the assessor determines that the minimum conformance standards have not been met, the assessor can terminate the assessment process or continue the evaluation for the purposes of developmental needs and to assist the organization in identifying specific areas that require improvements. In this case, regardless of the ultimate number of points scored, the schedule model assessment value will not be recorded on the continuum because it does not meet the minimum conformance standards.

5.2 Conformance Assessment Process

Appendix D contains a list of the schedule components organized into core required components (CRC), conditionally required components (RRC, ERC, KRC), and optional components. Table 5-1 reflects the maximum number of components by category as well as the total maximum scoreable number of components. The NS components are not included in this table so the total number of available components does not equal the total number of components defined in Chapter 4. Utilizing the list in Appendix D, the assessor will determine if each required component is present in the schedule model being analyzed. The scheduler should fully understand the good practices associated with the various required and optional components.

Table 5-1. Number of Components by Category

Required	Conditional			Optional	Total Available
CRC	RRC	ERC	KRC	Optional	
36	11	9	7	40	103

To begin the assessment process, the assessor will first determine the answer to the following questions:

- Is there a requirement for resource loading?

- Is there a requirement to utilize EVM?

- Is there a requirement to utilize schedule-based risk management?

- If the answer to any of the questions is yes, then the required schedule components for that group will be needed in addition to the CRC. The CRC, then, will be present in any schedule model. Examples of how the conditional required components may affect the threshold include:

- If resource loading is required, the RRC becomes required and the minimum level of required components is CRC + RRC.

- If EVM is required, the ERC becomes required, and the minimum level of required components is CRC + ERC.

- If risk management is required, the KRC becomes required, and the minimum level of required components is CRC + KRC.

- If both resource loading and EVM are required, the minimum level of required components is CRC + RRC + ERC.

- If resource loading, risk management and EVM are required, the minimum level of required components is CRC + KRC + RRC + ERC.

Depending on the project requirements, the value that can be attained for full compliance of the required components can vary between CRC and CRC plus the sum of additional components required by RRC / ERC / KRC. This value comprises the first part of the assessment process called the "required components value."

The remaining part of the assessment score is comprised of all the available "optional" components. For example, if KRC components are not required, then all risk components are considered optional. Once the required components are accounted for all of the remaining components are represented by the "optional components value." The assessor will review the remaining optional components and, if they are present and properly utilized, will award the points as indicated.

Each optional component also has a value of one. The assessor determines a raw score by summing all earned points from the required components and the optional components. If all of the points associated with the "required components value" are not earned, then a final raw score cannot be registered, however the raw score can be shared with the project so they can understand their areas for improvement. Finally, the raw score is divided by the total maximum possible score to obtain the conformance index. The resulting value is expressed as a percentage, and represents the conformance index score for the schedule model.

The basic intent of evaluating a schedule model's conformance with this practice standard and its implied maturity has been accomplished, and the assessor has determined where a given schedule model falls on the assessment continuum. The scheduler can then determine specific actions for moving farther along the continuum. A higher conformance index value does not automatically imply a better schedule model; however it may indicate a greater likelihood of achieving project objectives.

Appendix E contains a blank scoring sheet and some examples.

REFERENCES

[1] Project Management Institute. 2008. *A Guide to the Project Management Body of Knowledge (PMBOK® Guide)*—Fourth Edition. Newtown Square, PA: Author.

[2] Project Management Institute. 2007. *Practice Standard for Scheduling.* Newtown Square, PA: Author

[3] Project Management Institute. 2006. *Practice Standard for Work Breakdown Structures*—Second Edition. Newtown Square, PA: Author.

[4] Project Management Institute. 2005. *Practice Standard for Earned Value Management.* Newtown Square, PA: Author.

[5] Project Management Institute. 2011. *Practice Standard for Project Estimating.* Newtown Square, PA: Author.

[6] Project Management Institute. 2009. *Practice Standard for Project Risk Management.* Newtown Square, PA: Author.

[7] Project Management Institute. 2007. *Practice Standard for Configuration Management.* Newtown Square, PA: Author.

[8] Project Management Institute. 2008. *Organizational Project Management Maturity Model (OPM3)* Second Edition. Newtown Square, PA: Author.

APPENDIX A

GUIDELINES FOR A PROJECT MANAGEMENT INSTITUTE PRACTICE STANDARD

A.1 Introduction

A PMI practice standard is characterized as follow:

- Each practice standard provides guidelines on the mechanics (e.g., nuts and bolts, basics, fundamentals, step-by-step usage guide, how it operates, how to do it) of some significant process (input, tool, technique, or output) that is relevant to a project manager.

- A practice standard does not necessarily mirror the life-cycle phases of many projects. But, an individual practice standard may be applicable to the completion of one or more phases within a project.

- A practice standard does not necessarily mirror the Knowledge Areas within *A Guide to the Project Management Body of Knowledge (PMBOK® Guide)*, although an individual practice standard will provide sufficient detail and background for one or more of the inputs, tools and techniques, and/or outputs. Therefore, practice standards are not required to use the name of any Knowledge Area.

- Each practice standard should include information on *what* the significant process is and does, *why* it is significant, *how* to perform it, *when* it should be performed and, if necessary for further clarification, *who* should perform it.

- Each practice standard should include information that is accepted and applicable for most projects most of the time within the project management community. Processes that are generally restricted or applicable to one industry, country, or companion profession (i.e., an application area) may be included as an appendix for informational purposes, rather than part of the practice standard. With strong support and evidence, an application area-specific process may be considered as an *extension* practice standard, in the same manner as extensions to the *PMBOK® Guide* are considered.

- Each practice standard will benefit from the inclusion of examples and templates. It is best when an example or template includes a discussion of its strengths and weaknesses. A background description may be necessary to put this discussion in the appropriate context. The examples should be aligned with the relevant information in the standard or its appendix and placed in proximity to that information.

- All practice standards will be written in the same general style and format.

- Each practice standard project will assess the need to align with or reference other practice standards.

- Each practice standard will be consistent with the *PMBOK® Guide*.

- Each practice standard is intended to be more prescriptive than the *PMBOK® Guide*.

APPENDIX B

EVOLUTION OF PMI'S PRACTICE STANDARD FOR SCHEDULING

B.1 Pre-Project

The *Practice Standard for Scheduling* was initially published in 2007. In July 2009, the PMI Market Development Department conducted an Update Needs Survey for the practice standard, which is the preparatory step for chartering an update of any standard. In October 2009, the PMI Standards Manager and the Standards Member Advisory Group developed an initial charter for the update of the standard. A final version of the Charter was signed in January 2010. Per the charter, the committee was to review, investigate, validate the need, and identify all necessary changes to update the *Practice Standard for Scheduling* as a second-edition standard.

Specific activities included:

- Consideration of all comments and feedback relevant to the *Practice Standard for Scheduling* that have been received by PMI since publication

- Consideration of all deferred Exposure Draft comments, suggestions, and feedback, including any appeals and their resolution, with the assistance of PMI staff

- Consideration of any available PMI market research data and information

- Consideration of any available data and information

- Consideration of initiating *ad hoc* research to resolve issues

- Consideration of consultation with subject matter experts

- Consideration of impacts from and to other standards products

- Implement the syntax change to the PMI standards format, that is, verb-noun for process names

- Consideration of recommendation for changes, for no changes (reaffirmation), or to retire the standard

- Assembly of the Committee's summary findings and recommendations in a comprehensive report to the Standards Manager

In January 2010, the committee was formed under the leadership of Harold "Mike" Mosley, Jr., PMP, Chair, and Charles Follin, PMP, Vice-Chair.

B.2 Preliminary Work

With the formation of the committee, PMI supplied a list of volunteers. A matrix was developed to make every effort to address the qualifications and geographic distribution of the committee membership. A set of interviews was conducted to evaluate the range of volunteers, including to determine if they had any specific agendas they were pursuing through this opportunity. A committee of eight members was determined to be optimal and the following metrics were achieved:

B.2.1 Qualifications:

- Eight PMP
- Five PMP-SP
- One PMI-RMP

B.2.2 Geographic:

- Five–North America (four states, coast to coast)
- One–EMEA (Lithuania)
- Two–Asia Pacific (Israel and India)
- Two–Latin America (Curacao & Brazil)

Note—This totals more than eight as there was movement of the members during the course of the effort.

B.2.3 Market:

- Five–Consulting (construction, technology, program)
- One–Construction
- One–Finance/Automotive
- One–IT/Software

B.2.4 Applications:

- Artemis
- Finest Hour
- Maximo
- MicroPlanner
- MS Office Project
- Open Plan Professional

- Oracle P6

- PERTmaster

- Parade

- Primavera Project Planner (P3)

- Project Two

- PS-Next

- Risk+

- RiskyProject

- SureTrak

- @Task

This composition provided for a highly diverse team, optimizing the perspective in development, the applicability in implementation, and the translatability of the completed standard. In February 2010, the team had its initial opportunity to engage in the effort. Lead by Mike Mosley (Chair) and Charlie Follin (Vice-Chair), the committee included Jim Aksel, Bridget Fleming, Hagit Landman, Sanjay Mandhan, Fernando Oliveira, Raul Romer, and Elaine Lazar (PMI Standards Specialist).

Initial efforts included the consultation with various subject matter experts seeking input on what areas needed to be addressed in the update of this *Practice Standard for Scheduling.* This feedback led to the expansion of the standard to better inclusion of earned value techniques, resource application, and risk management.

The committee also established liaison with other standards in concurrent, or nearly concurrent, development. These included the Practice Standard for Earned Value Management 2nd Edition, The Practice Standard for Project Estimating, the *PMBOK®* Guide—Fifth Edition, and the Lexicon Committee. In addition, there was a focus to understand and strive for harmony between the Practice Standard for Scheduling and other published standards, such as the Practice Standard for Project Risk Management and the charter mandated *PMBOK®* Guide—Fourth Edition. This effort also included the review and consideration of the exam specification for the PMI-SP exam.

The committee development efforts ran from February through August of 2010. During this period there were three face-to-face meetings where great progress was made through "dynamic dialog," with each person's passion being expressed in the effort to learn and ultimately to reach consensus on a team approach. One of these meetings was coordinated to be in conjunction with the PMI College of Scheduling Sixth Annual Conference, where a session was held as a pseudo-standards open working session. Committee members also presented at the American Nuclear Society's Utility Working Conference, and at the PMI Global Congress North America 2010. Mike Mosley also continued his role of liaison with the PMI College of Scheduling (now the Scheduling Community of Practice), reporting to the Board and posting updates on the community website. Along with the College's website forum, several new venues were engaged in the collaboration and discussion of the standard, including social networking sites.

There are probably two issues that seem to continue to draw comments:

- Ever since the term "schedule model" was introduced in the *PMBOK® Guide*—Third Edition, there has been dialog about the need for a new term. After both internal and external dynamic dialog, the committee still agrees with the need for terms that are specific to what is being requested. In common usage, a schedule is everything from a list of date to a mathematical model that can replicate the planned execution of a project. The terms used in the standard provide an owner, team member, or scheduler the opportunity to be specific as to need and expectations.

- The definition of "critical" has also spurred conversation, mostly in relation to its traditional usage, only considering the single longest path through a project and its constituents. With the usage of constraints, multiple calendars, and multiple subprojects in most projects, it is very common to have multiple critical paths based on manager/subproject, area, or contractual obligations.

The *Practice Standard for Scheduling*—Second Edition offers the community a broader scope, increased clarity, and an even higher level of consensus. The components list offered the building blocks supportive of creating a schedule model, good practices for their use and a means to evaluate the maturity of the schedule model against the needs of the project.

B.3 Exposure and Consensus

This practice standard was submitted as an exposure draft in the late fall of 2010. There were 867 comments. The team's comment acceptance rate (comments accepted outright or accepted with modifications) was at a near record high of 85.6%. Only 0.6% (six of 867) of the comments were deferred to a future edition and only 3% were rejected. Those comments that were related to format or punctuation were referred to the PMI editor for style guide interpretation.

APPENDIX C

CONTRIBUTORS AND REVIEWERS OF THE *PRACTICE STANDARD FOR SCHEDULING*—SECOND EDITION

This appendix lists, alphabetically within groupings, those individuals who have contributed to the development and production of the *Practice Standard for Scheduling*—Second Edition.

The Project Management Institute is grateful to all of these individuals for their support and acknowledges their contributions to the project management profession.

C.1 Core Committee

The following individuals served as members, were contributors of text or concepts, and served as leaders on the Committee:

Harold "Mike" Mosley, Jr., PMP, P.E., Chair
Charles T. Follin, PMP, Vice Chair
M. Elaine Lazar, MA, MA, AStd, PMI Standards Project Specialist
James E. Aksel, PMP, PMI-SP
Bridget Fleming, PMP, PMI-SP
Hagit Landman, PMP, PMI-SP, MBA
Sanjay Mandhan, MBA, PMP
Fernando Nunes de Oliveira, PMP, PMI-SP, PMI-RMP
Raul A. Römer, Ing., PMP, PMI-SP

C.2 Significant Contributors

Significant contributors supported key activities for the update to this practice standard including editing and subteam participation in project efforts such as content, authoring, quality, communications and research subteams. The update project's significant contributors offered depth of knowledge and insight as subject matter experts (SMEs) in their fields of practice. In addition to the members of the project core team, the following individuals provided significant support, input or concepts:

Doug Clark
Marie Gunnerson
Tammo Wilkins
David T. Hulett, PhD

C.3 Exposure Draft Reviewers and Contributors

In addition to team members, the following individuals provided recommendations for improving the *Practice Standard for Scheduling*—Second Edition:

Marcos Abreu	Mohammad Abu Irshaid
Puneet Agrawal	Imran Ahmed
James Aksel	Jose Alcala
Eric Amo	Balamurugan Ananthan
Ondiappan Arivazhagan	Sai Prasad Baba Subramanyan
Stephen Bonk	John Buxton
Kameswaran Chandrasekaran	Supriyo Chatterji
Cynthia Datte	Kian Ghadaksaz
David Giguere	Peter Gilliland
Behnam Goudarzi	Roy Greenia
Nitu Gupta	Miklos Hajdu
George Haney	Ahmed Hasan
Sheriff Hashem	Lee Hindsman
Shirley Hinton	Abdelkader Ibrahim
Mohamed Ishaq	Ashok Jain
Jacob Jerome	Ashish Joshi
Chandrashekhar Joshi	Carl Karshagen
Ramakrishna Kavirayani	Edward Kleinert
Anuj Kulkarni	Marina Link
Bruce Lofland	Jose Machicao
Ramesh Maddali	Mohit Mathur
Amith Mikkilineni	Samit Misra
Shamik Mondal	Balu Muthusamy
Eric Myers	Harishchandra Nayak
Shashank Neppalli	Mohammad Ali Niroomand Rad
Sunil Omanakuttan	Venkateswar Oruganti
Vincent Osbourn	Boopathy Sankar P S
Madhuyukta Pandey	Balaji Pasupathy
Valikulangara Pradeepkumar	Ananthakrishnan Ramaswami
Bhaskar Ravivarma	Bhavanam Reddy
Michael Reed	Sadegh Roozbehi
Himadri Roy	Sameer Siddhanti
Gurpreet Singh	Justin Smith
Manish Srivastava	Goparaju Sudhakar
Mark Swiderski	Seyedsoroush Tabatabaei

Biagio Tramontana
Vijay Vemana
Atin Wadehra
Kevin Wegryn

Eric Uyttewaal
David Violette
Patrick Weaver
Alexandra Zouncourides-Lull

C.4 Other Contributors

Mark Groff
Gwen Barger
Peter Ripley
Jeff Goodman

C.5 PMI Standards Program Member Advisory Group (MAG)

The following individuals served as members of the PMI Standards Program Member Advisory Group during development of the *Practice Standard for Scheduling*—Second Edition:

Monique Aubry, PhD, MPM
Margareth F.S. Carneiro, MSc, PMP
Chris Cartwright, MPM, PMP
Terry Cooke-Davies, PhD, BA, FAPM, FCMI, FRSA, PMP
Laurence Goldsmith, PMP
David W. Ross, PMP, PgMP
Paul E. Shaltry, PMP
John Zlockie, MBA, PMP, Standards Manager

C.6 Production Staff

Special mention is due to the following employees of PMI:

Donn Greenberg, Publications Manager
Roberta Storer, Product Editor
Barbara Walsh, CAPM, Publications Production Supervisor
Quynh Woodward, MBA, Standards Compliance Specialist

APPENDIX D

CONFORMANCE ASSESSMENT SCORING TABLE

Table D-1 provides additional clarity concerning the four component categories: core required components (CRC), conditionally required components (RRC, ERC, KRC) and optional components. The components are arranged in the table according to when the component might be used in accordance with typical schedule model evolutions; Pre-Development, Development and Maintenance. This table also provides the basis for the official count of each component category that is used in the assessment worksheet, shown in Appendix E.

The component is listed in the first column on the left of the table. The next five columns show which category the component falls into; required core components (CRC), conditional resource components (RRC), conditional EVM components (ERC), conditional risk components (KRC), or optional components (OPT). The last line of the table reflects a summary of each category type with a total value for the components. This last summary line is also reflected on the top of the assessment worksheet as a reminder of the total available points in each category.

Table D-1. Sample Conformance Assessment Scoring Table

Component	CRC	RRC	ERC	KRC	OPT	Comments
WBS ID			R			
Activity ID	R					
Project Name	R					
Schedule Model ID	R					
Schedule Model Version	R					
Activity Calendar					O	
Project Calendar	R					
Resource Calendar		R				
Data Date	R					
Milestones	R					
Lag					O	
Baseline Schedule Model	R					
Target Schedule Model					O	

Table D-1. Sample Conformance Assessment Scoring Table *(Continued)*

Component	CRC	RRC	ERC	KRC	OPT	Comments
Project Start Constraint					0	
Activity Label	R					
Unit of Measure	R					
Activity Original Duration	R					
Activity Remaining Duration	R					
Activity Actual Duration	R					
Activity Total Duration	R					
Project Remaining Duration	R					
Project Actual Duration	R					
Project Total Duration	R					
Activity Effort/Work					0	
Activity Work Percent Complete					0	
Finish to Start	R					
Start to Start					0	
Finish to Finish					0	
Activity Early Start Date	R					
Activity Late Start Date	R					
Activity Actual Start Date	R					
Activity Resource Leveled Start Date					0	
Project Early Start Date	R					
Project Late Start Date	R					
Project Actual Start Date	R					
Project Resource Leveled Start Date					0	
Activity Early Finish Date	R					
Activity Late Finish Date	R					
Activity Actual Finish Date	R					
Activity Resource Leveled Finish Date					0	
Project Early Finish Date	R					
Project Late Finish Date	R					
Project Actual Finish Date	R					

Table D-1. Sample Conformance Assessment Scoring Table (Continued)

Component	CRC	RRC	ERC	KRC	OPT	Comments
Project Resource Leveled Finish Date					0	
Total Float	R					
Free Float	R					
Critical Path	R					
Activity Physical Percent Complete	R					Activity percent complete must be either physical OR duration - ONE is required
Activity Duration Percent Complete						Activity percent complete must be either physical OR duration - ONE is required
Project Physical Percent Complete	R					Activity percent complete must be either physical OR duration - ONE is required
Project Duration Percent Complete						Activity percent complete must be either physical OR duration - ONE is required
Activity Code					0	
Activity Cost Category					0	
Activity Cost Estimate					0	
Activity Resource Actual Quantity		R				
Activity Resource Total Quantity		R				
Project Resource Actual Quantity		R				
Project Resource Total Quantity		R				
Activity Scope Definition					0	
Finish Not Later Than					0	
Project Finish Constraint					0	
Custom Field					0	
Earned Value			R			
Planned Value			R			
Activity Actual Cost (AC)			R			
Cost Performance Index (CPI)					0	
Schedule Performance index (SPI)					0	
To Complete Performance Index (TCPI)					0	

Table D-1. Sample Conformance Assessment Scoring Table *(Continued)*

Component	CRC	RRC	ERC	KRC	OPT	Comments
Schedule Variance (SV)					0	
Schedule Variance %					0	
Cost Variance (CV)					0	
Cost Variance %					0	
Earned Value Method					0	
Earned Value Weight					0	
Work Package Identifier			R			
Control Account ID			R			
Control Account Manager					0	
Estimate at Completion (EAC)			R			
Budget at Completion (BAC)			R			
Estimate to Complete (ETC)			R			
Change Request Identifier					0	
Project Schedule Level					0	
Project Schedule Presentation	R					
Project Cost Category					0	
Project Description					0	
Project Manager					0	
Resource Assignment		R				
Resource Availability		R				
Resource Description		R				
Driving Resources					0	
Resource ID		R				
Resource Lag					0	
Resource Leveling					0	
Resource Library/ Dictionary		R				
Resource Rates/Prices					0	
Resource Type		R				
Activity Risk Criticality Index				R		
Risk ID				R		

Table D-1. Sample Conformance Assessment Scoring Table *(Continued)*

Component	CRC	RRC	ERC	KRC	OPT	Comments
Activity Most Likely Duration				R		
Activity Optimistic Duration				R		
Activity Pessimistic Duration				R		
Activity Cumulative Probability Risk Distribution				R		
Probability Risk Distribution				R		
Summary Activity					0	
Variance					0	
Number of Components in Category	36	11	9	7	40	NS items are not counted in OPT

103

APPENDIX E

CONFORMANCE ASSESSMENT WORKSHEETS

Appendix E provides a number of assessment worksheets. Each worksheet is explained in greater detail below. The values used for the total counts in each component category are taken directly from Appendix D.

Figure E-1 reflects the potentially available values for each category filled in. Note that the conditional component categories are listed in both sections at this point since it has not been determined yet if they are required for the given project. The base sheet also reflects the required value for the core components, the available optional values and at the bottom of the page the total available points is shown. This base sheet can be reproduced and manually marked up for any assessment.

Figure E-2 reflects a completed worksheet for a project that only required resource loading in addition to the base core components and reflects the presence of some optional components as well. The example reflects an assessment score of 55.

Figure E-3 reflects a completed worksheet for a project that requires resource loading, EVM and risk management in addition to the base core components and reflects the presence of some optional components as well. The example reflects an assessment score of 70.

Figure E-4 reflects a completed worksheet for a project that required resource loading and risk management in addition to the base core components and reflects the presence of some optional components as well. The example reflects an assessment score of 90. Note that some of the scored optional components are the EVM components, but since they were not required on this project they are in the optional category.

Figure E-5 reflects a completed worksheet for a project that required resource loading and risk management in addition to the base core components and reflects the presence of some optional components as well, including all of the EVM components. However, you will note that this assessment has no score, because not all of the required components are present. Three of the core requirements are missing as well as three of the resource components. The rules state that if the required components are not present, then no score shall be recorded. Note you can still see earned versus available points in both the required and optional areas, but no conformance index value is recorded.

Appendix E was developed to provide the user with examples for greater understanding of how the assessment process works.

Figure E-1. Base Worksheet

SCHEDULE ASSESSMENT WORKSHEET

Required	Conditional			Optional	Total
CRC	RRC	ERC	KRC	Optional	Available
36	11	9	7	40	103

Assessment Questions:

		Yes	No
1	Is there a requirement for resource loading?		
2	Is there a requirement to utilize EVM?		
3	Is there a requirement to utilize risk management?		

The answers to the above questions will determine the values for the available points for the required and optional components to be placed in the fields below. The CRC is always required so additional required values from the chart above will be added to the CRC to obtain the total available required points. All remaining categories become optional by definition and that value is recorded as the optional value. The total available will always equal the value of 103.

Required Components Score

	Potential Available	Required	EARNED		
Core Required Components (CRC)	36	36		Required Points	
Resource Required Components (RRC)	11				
EVM Required Components (ERC)	9			Earned Points	
Risk Required Components (KRC)	7				
Total Required Components					

Optional Components Score

	Potential Available	Available Optional	EARNED		
Optional Components	40	40		Available Points	
Resource Required Components	11				
EVM Required Components	9			Earned Points	
Risk Required Components	7				
Total Optional Components					

Total Score

This box only completed if ALL required points are earned

Required Components Score		
Optional Components Score		
	Total	

Total Available Points	103

Total Earned	
Total Points	103

Raw Conformance Index Value ☐

Multiply by 100   100

Conformance Index ☐

Figure E-2. Resource Required Example Worksheet

SCHEDULE ASSESSMENT WORKSHEET

Required	Conditional			Optional	Total
CRC	RRC	ERC	KRC	Optional	Available
36	11	9	7	40	103

Assessment Questions:

		Yes	No
1	Is there a requirement for resource loading?	X	
2	Is there a requirement to utilize EVM?		X
3	Is there a requirement to utilize risk management?		X

The answers to the above questions will determine the values for the available points for the required and optional components to be placed in the fields below. The CRC is always required so additional required values from the chart above will be added to the CRC to obtain the total available required points. All remaining categories become optional by definition and that value is recorded as the optional value. The total available will always equal the value of 103.

Required Components Score

	Potential Available	Required	EARNED		
Core Required Components (CRC)	36	36	36	Required Points	47
Resource Required Components (RRC)	11	11	11		
EVM Required Components (ERC)	9	0		Earned Points	47
Risk Required Components (KRC)	7	0			
Total Required Components		47	47		

Optional Components Score

	Potential Available	Available Optional	EARNED		
Optional Components	40	40	5	Available Points	56
Resource Required Components	11	0			
EVM Required Components	9	9	5	Earned Points	10
Risk Required Components	7	7			
Total Optional Components		56	10		

Total Score

This box only completed if ALL required points are earned

Required Components Score		47	Total Available Points	103
Optional Components Score		10		
	Total	57		

Total Earned	57	
Total Points	103	

Raw Conformance Index Value	0.55
Multiply by 100	100

Conformance Index	55

Figure E-3. Resource, EVM and Risk Required Example Worksheet

SCHEDULE ASSESSMENT WORKSHEET

Required	Conditional			Optional	Total
CRC	RRC	ERC	KRC	Optional	Available
36	11	9	7	40	103

Assessment Questions:

		Yes	No
1	Is there a requirement for resource loading?	X	
2	Is there a requirement to utilize EVM?	X	
3	Is there a requirement to utilize risk management?	X	

The answers to the above questions will determine the values for the available points for the required and optional components to be placed in the fields below. The CRC is always required so additional required values from the chart above will be added to the CRC to obtain the total available required points. All remaining categories become optional by definition and that value is recorded as the optional value. The total available will always equal the value of 103.

Required Components Score

	Potential Available	Required	EARNED		
Core Required Components (CRC)	36	36	36	Required Points	63
Resource Required Components (RRC)	11	11	11		
EVM Required Components (ERC)	9	9	9	Earned Points	63
Risk Required Components (KRC)	7	7	7		
Total Required Components		63	63		

Optional Components Score

	Potential Available	Available Optional	EARNED		
Optional Components	40	40	9	Available Points	40
Resource Required Components	11	0			
EVM Required Components	9	0		Earned Points	9
Risk Required Components	7	0			
Total Optional Components		40	9		

Total Score

This box only completed if ALL required points are earned

Required Components Score	63	
Optional Components Score	9	
	Total	72

Total Available Points	103

Total Earned	72
Total Points	103

Raw Conformance Index Value	0.70
Multiply by 100	100
Conformance Index	**70**

Figure E-4. Resource and Risk Required Example Worksheet

SCHEDULE ASSESSMENT WORKSHEET

Required	Conditional			Optional	Total
CRC	RRC	ERC	KRC	Optional	Available
36	11	9	7	40	103

Assessment Questions:

		Yes	No
1	Is there a requirement for resource loading?	X	
2	Is there a requirement to utilize EVM?		X
3	Is there a requirement to utilize risk management?	X	

The answers to the above questions will determine the values for the available points for the required and optional components to be placed in the fields below. The CRC is always required so additional required values from the chart above will be added to the CRC to obtain the total available required points. All remaining categories become optional by definition and that value is recorded as the optional value. The total available will always equal the value of 103.

Required Components Score

	Potential Available	Required	EARNED		
Core Required Components (CRC)	36	36	36	Required Points	54
Resource Required Components (RRC)	11	11	11		
EVM Required Components (ERC)	9	0		Earned Points	54
Risk Required Components (KRC)	7	7	7		
Total Required Components		54	54		

Optional Components Score

	Potential Available	Available Optional	EARNED		
Optional Components	40	40	30	Available Points	49
Resource Required Components	11	0			
EVM Required Components	9	9	9	Earned Points	39
Risk Required Components	7	0			
Total Optional Components		54	54		

Total Score

This box only completed if ALL required points are earned

				Total Available Points	103
Required Components Score		54			
Optional Components Score		39			
	Total	93			

Total Earned	93
Total Points	103

Raw Conformance Index Value	0.90
Multiply by 100	100

Conformance Index	90

Figure E-5. Non Scored Example Worksheet

SCHEDULE ASSESSMENT WORKSHEET

Required	Conditional			Optional	Total
CRC	RRC	ERC	KRC	Optional	Available
36	11	9	7	40	103

NOTE IN THIS EXAMPLE THE MINIMUM REQUIRED COMPONENTS WERE NOT ALL PRESENT

Assessment Questions:		Yes	No
1	Is there a requirement for resource loading?	X	
2	Is there a requirement to utilize EVM?		X
3	Is there a requirement to utilize risk management?	X	

The answers to the above questions will determine the values for the available points for the required and optional components to be placed in the fields below. The CRC is always required so additional required values from the chart above will be added to the CRC to obtain the total available required points. All remaining categories become optional by definition and that value is recorded as the optional value. The total available will always equal the value of 103.

Required Components Score

	Potential Available	Required	EARNED		
Core Required Components (CRC)	36	36	33	Required Points	54
Resource Required Components (RRC)	11	11	7		
EVM Required Components (ERC)	9	0		Earned Points	47
Risk Required Components (KRC)	7	7	7		
Total Required Components		54	47		

Optional Components Score

	Potential Available	Available Optional	EARNED		
Optional Components	40	40	25	Available Points	49
Resource Required Components	11	0			
EVM Required Components	9	9	9	Earned Points	34
Risk Required Components	7	0			
Total Optional Components		49	34		

Total Score

This box only completed if ALL required points are earned

Required Components Score	
Optional Components Score	
	Total

Total Available Points	103

Total Earned	81
Total Points	103

Raw Conformance Index Value	
Multiply by 100	100
Conformance Index	

GLOSSARY

Many of the words defined here have broader, and in some cases, different dictionary definitions.

The definitions use the following conventions:

- Terms used as part of the definitions and that are defined in the glossary are shown in *italics*.

  - When the same glossary term appears more than once in a given definition, only the first occurrence is italicized.

  - In some cases, a single glossary term consists of multiple words (e.g. control account).

- When synonyms are included, no definition is given and the reader is directed to the preferred term (i.e., see preferred term).

- Related terms that are not synonyms are cross-referenced at the end of the definition (i.e., see also related term).

Common Acronyms and Terms

Acronym	Term
AC	Actual Cost
	Use Actual Cost (AC) (*PMBOK® Guide*—Fourth Edition)
AD	Activity Description
	Use Activity Description (AD) (*PMBOK® Guide*—Fourth Edition)
ADM	Arrow Diagramming Method
	Use Arrow Diagramming Method (ADM) (*PMBOK® Guide*—Fourth Edition)
AF	Actual Finish Date
	Use Actual Finish Date (AF) (*PMBOK® Guide*—Fourth Edition)
AOA	Activity-on-Arrow (*PMBOK® Guide*—Fourth Edition)
AON	Activity-on-Node (*PMBOK® Guide*—Fourth Edition)
AS	Actual Start Date
	Use Actual Start Date (AS) (*PMBOK® Guide*—Fourth Edition)
CA	Control Account
	Use Control Account (CA) (*PMBOK® Guide*—Fourth Edition)
CPM	Critical Path Method
	Use Critical Path Method (CPM) (*PMBOK® Guide*—Fourth Edition)

DD	Data Date
	Use Data Date (DD) (*PMBOK® Guide*—Fourth Edition)
DU	Duration
	Use Duration (DU or DUR) (*PMBOK® Guide*—Fourth Edition)
DUR	Duration
	Use Duration (DU or DUR) (*PMBOK® Guide*—Fourth Edition)
EAC	Estimate at Completion
	Use Estimate at Completion (EAC) (*PMBOK® Guide*—Fourth Edition)
EF	Early Finish Date
	Use Early Finish Date (EF) (*PMBOK® Guide*—Fourth Edition)
ES	Early Start Date
	Use Early Start Date (ES) (*PMBOK® Guide*—Fourth Edition)
ETC	Estimate to Complete
	Use Estimate to Complete (ETC) (*PMBOK® Guide*—Fourth Edition)
EV	Earned Value
	Use Earned Value (EV) (*PMBOK® Guide*—Fourth Edition)
EVM	Earned Value Management
	Use Earned Value Management (EVM) (*PMBOK® Guide*—Fourth Edition)
EVT	Earned Value Technique
	Use Earned Value Technique (EVT) (*PMBOK® Guide*—Fourth Edition)
FF	Finish-to-Finish
	Use Finish-to-Finish (FF) (*PMBOK® Guide*—Fourth Edition)
FF	Free Float
	Use Free Float (FF) (*PMBOK® Guide*—Fourth Edition)
FS	Finish-to-Start
	Use Finish-to-Start (FS) (*PMBOK® Guide*—Fourth Edition)
LF	Late Finish Date
	Use Late Finish Date (LF) (*PMBOK® Guide*—Fourth Edition)
LS	Late Start Date
	Use Late Start Date (LS) (*PMBOK® Guide*—Fourth Edition)
OD	Original Duration
	Use Original Duration (OD) (*PMBOK® Guide*—Fourth Edition)

PC   Percent Complete

Use Percent Complete (PC or PCT) (*PMBOK® Guide*—Fourth Edition)

PCT   Percent Complete

Use Percent Complete (PC or PCT) (*PMBOK® Guide*—Fourth Edition)

PDM   Precedence Diagramming Method

Use Precedence Diagramming Method (PDM) (*PMBOK® Guide*—Fourth Edition)

PF   Planned Finish Date (*PMBOK® Guide*—Fourth Edition)

PM   Project Manager

Use Project Manager (PM) (*PMBOK® Guide*—Fourth Edition)

PMB   Performance Measurement Baseline

Use Performance Measurement Baseline (PMB) (*PMBOK® Guide*—Fourth Edition)

PMO   Project Management Office

Use Project Management Office (PMO) (*PMBOK® Guide*—Fourth Edition)

PS   Planned Start Date (*PMBOK® Guide*—Fourth Edition)

RD   Remaining Duration

Use Remaining Duration (RD) (*PMBOK® Guide*—Fourth Edition)

SF   Scheduled Finish Date

Use Scheduled Finish Date (SF) (*PMBOK® Guide*—Fourth Edition)

SF   Start-to-Finish

Use Start-to-Finish (SF) (*PMBOK® Guide*—Fourth Edition)

SOW   Statement of Work

Use Statement of Work (SOW) (*PMBOK® Guide*—Fourth Edition)

SS   Scheduled Start Date

Use Scheduled Start Date (SS) (*PMBOK® Guide*—Fourth Edition)

SS   Start-to-Start

Use Start-to-Start (SS) (*PMBOK® Guide*—Fourth Edition)

SV   Schedule Variance

Use Schedule Variance (SV) (*PMBOK® Guide*—Fourth Edition)

TF   Target Finish Date

Use Target Finish Date (TF) (*PMBOK® Guide*—Fourth Edition)

TF   Total Float

Use Total Float (TF) (*PMBOK® Guide*—Fourth Edition)

TS   Target Start Date

UsE Target Start Date (TS) (**PMBOK® Guide—Fourth Edition**)

WBS   Work Breakdown Structure

UsE Work Breakdown Structure (WBS) (**PMBOK® Guide—Fourth Edition**)

Terms and Definitions

Activity. A component of work performed during the course of a project. See also *schedule activity*.

Activity Actual Cost. The total cost of the work completed during a given time period. This value may be calculated at any schedule model outline level and between various data dates. If the calculation is performed using the project start date and the most current data date, the values are called "cumulative."

Activity Actual Duration. The total number of work periods in calendar units between the activity actual start date of the schedule activity and either the data date of the schedule model, if the schedule activity is in progress, or the activity actual finish date, if the schedule activity is complete. See also *actual duration*.

Activity Actual Finish Date. The point in time at which a schedule activity is completed. See also *actual finish date*.

Activity Actual Start Date. The point in time at which a schedule activity began.

Activity Attributes [Output/Input]. Multiple attributes associated with each schedule activity that can be included within the activity list. Activity attributes include activity codes, predecessor activities, successor activities, logical relationships, leads and lags, resource requirements, imposed dates, constraints, and assumptions.

Activity Baseline Finish Date. The point in time associated with the completion of the *schedule* activity in an approved project schedule baseline. See also *activity current finish date*.

Activity Baseline Duration. The total number of work periods in calendar units between the activity baseline start date and activity baseline finish date of a schedule activity as determined by its approved project schedule baseline.

Activity Baseline Start Date. The point in time associated with the beginning of the schedule activity in an approved project schedule baseline. See also *activity current start date*.

Activity Box. A graphic object used to display schedule activity data in accordance with schedule network logic.

Activity Calendar. Usually the project calendar, or another specifically defined calendar from the calendar library, assigned to the schedule activity which defines the work periods and non-work periods in calendar format. The activity calendar, on the schedule activities to which it is assigned, is used to replace the project calendar during schedule network analysis. See also *calendar library*.

Activity Code. One or more numerical or text values that identify characteristics of the work or in some way categorize the schedule activity that allows filtering and ordering of activities within reports.

Activity Cost Estimate. The projected cost of the schedule activity that includes the cost for all resources required to perform and complete the activity, including all cost types and cost components.

Activity Cumulative Probability Risk Distribution. A table of dates and their associated cumulative probabilities of occurrence for schedule activity completion. Dates are derived using analytical techniques such as Monte Carlo calculations. When applied to the project end date, the value is equivalent to the project cumulative probability risk distribution.

Activity Current Finish Date. The current estimate of the point in time when the schedule activity will be completed, where the estimate reflects any reported work progress. See also *activity scheduled finish date, activity baseline finish date, current finish date.*

Activity Current Start Date. The current estimate of the point in time when the schedule activity will begin, where the estimate reflects any reported work progress. See also *activity scheduled start date, activity baseline start date, and current start date.*

Activity Description (AD). A short phrase or label for each schedule activity, used in conjunction with an activity identifier to differentiate a project schedule activity from other schedule activities. The activity description normally identifies the scope of work of the schedule activity. Also known as activity name or activity title.

Define Activities [Process]. The process of identifying the specific schedule activities that need to be performed to produce the various project deliverables.

Estimate Activity Durations [Process]. The process of estimating the number of work periods that will be needed to complete individual schedule activities.

Activity Duration. The total number of work periods, in calendar units, between the activity early start date and the activity early finish date of a schedule activity. See also *Duration* (DU or DUR).

Activity Duration Percent Complete. The calculated percentage that the activity actual duration is of the activity total duration for a schedule activity that has work in progress.

Activity Duration Variance. A quantifiable deviation, departure, or divergence away from a given duration for a schedule activity.

Activity Expected Finish Date. A date constraint placed on both the activity early and late finish dates of an in-progress schedule activity that affects when the schedule activity can be scheduled for completion and is usually in the form of a fixed imposed date. This constraint requires the activity remaining duration to be set equal to the difference between the activity expected finish date and the data date to force the schedule activity to be scheduled to finish upon the imposed date.

Activity Early Finish Date. The earliest possible point in time when the uncompleted portion of the schedule activity can be completed given the assigned resources. See also *early finish date.*

Activity Early Start Date. The earliest possible point in time when the schedule activity can begin based on the CPM forward pass of schedule model logic. See also *early start date*.

Activity Finish Date. A point in time associated with the completion of a schedule activity in a project. Usually qualified by one of the following: actual, baseline, current, early, expected, late, mandatory, scheduled, or target. See also *finish date*.

Activity Group. A project team member-selected set of schedule activities, sharing some common activity attribute that allows the activities to be grouped and reported or displayed separately, such as being divided in a graphic display from other activities with a horizontal line.

Activity Identifier. A short unique numeric or text identification assigned to each schedule activity to differentiate that project activity from other activities. Typically unique within any one schedule model network diagram.

Activity Label. A short phrase or label for each schedule activity used in conjunction with an activity identifier to differentiate that schedule model activity from other schedule activities. The activity description normally describes the scope of work of the schedule activity. Also known as activity name or task name.

Activity Late Finish Date. The latest possible point in time when the schedule activity can be completed without violating a schedule constraint or delaying the project end date. See also *late finish date*.

Activity Late Start Date. The latest possible point in time when the schedule activity can begin without violating a schedule constraint or delaying the project end date. See also *late start date*.

Activity List [Output/Input]. A documented tabulation of schedule activities that shows the activity description, activity identifier, and a sufficiently detailed activity scope definition for the work so project team members understand what work is to be performed. The list may have additional activity attributes.

Activity Mandatory Finish Date. A finish date constraint placed on a schedule activity that sets both the activity early and late finish dates equal to a fixed imposed date and thereby also constrains the early start dates of the network paths logically following that schedule activity.

Activity Mandatory Start Date. A start date constraint placed on a schedule activity that set both the activity early and late start dates equal to a fixed imposed date and thereby also constrains the late finish date of the network paths logically preceding that schedule activity.

Activity Name. See *activity description*.

Activity Original Duration. The activity duration originally assigned to a schedule activity, this duration is typically not updated as progress is reported on the activity. Used for comparison with activity actual duration and activity remaining duration when reporting schedule progress. The activity original duration is normally developed by reliance on historic data, specialists, resource availability, financial considerations, and volume of work to be performed. May also be called planned duration.

Activity-on-Arrow (AOA). See *arrow diagramming method* (ADM).

Activity-on-Node (AON). See *precedence diagramming method* (PDM)

Activity Physical Percent Complete. An estimate, expressed as a percent, of the amount of work that has been completed on a schedule activity, measured in terms of either physical work progress or by means of the earning rules of earned value management.

Activity Planned Finish Date. See *activity scheduled finish date.*

Activity Planned Start Date. See *activity scheduled start date.*

Activity Remaining Duration. The total number of work periods in calendar units, (a) equal to the original duration for an activity that has not started or (b) between the data date of the project schedule and the CPM early finish date of a schedule activity that has an activity actual start date. This represents the time needed to complete a schedule activity where the work is in progress. See also *remaining duration.*

Estimate Activity Resources [Process]. The process of estimating the types and quantities of resources required to perform each schedule activity.

Activity Resource Leveled Finish Date. The point in time associated with the activity scheduled finish date of a resource limited schedule activity in a resource-limited schedule.

Activity Resource Leveled Start Date. The point in time associated with the activity scheduled start date of a resource limited schedule activity in a resource-limited schedule.

Activity Risk Criticality Index. The probability that the schedule activity will be on a critical path.

Activity Scheduled Finish Date. The point in time when work was scheduled to complete on a schedule activity. The activity schedule finish date is normally within the range of dates delimited by the activity early finish date and the activity late finish date. It may reflect resource leveling of scarce resources. Also known as activity planned finish date. See also *activity current finish date, scheduled finish date.*

Activity Scheduled Start Date. The point in time when work was scheduled to begin on a schedule activity. The activity schedule start date is normally within the range of dates delimited by the activity early start date and the activity late start date. It may reflect resource leveling of scarce resources. Also known as activity planned start date. See also *activity current start date, scheduled start date.*

Activity Scope Definition. Documented narrative describing the work represented by the activity.

Sequence Activities [Process]. The process of identifying and documenting dependencies among schedule activities.

Activity Start Date. A point in time associated with the beginning of the schedule activity in a project. Usually qualified by one of the following: actual, baseline, current, early, late, scheduled, or target. See also *start date.*

Activity Target Date Variance. A quantifiable deviation, departure, or divergence away from a known activity target start date or activity target finish date.

Activity Target Duration. The estimated total number of work periods in calendar units, needed to complete the schedule activity as determined by a specific project target schedule.

Activity Target Finish Date. A point in time established by schedule network analysis for completion of a schedule activity within a specific version of the project schedule.

Activity Target Start Date. A point in time established by schedule network analysis for beginning the schedule activity within a specific version of the project schedule.

Activity Title. See *activity description.*

Activity Total Duration. The total number of work periods in calendar units to complete a schedule activity. For schedule activities in progress, it includes the activity actual duration plus the activity remaining duration.

Activity Type. A categorization designation that differentiates the discrete schedule activities that have different functions within the schedule model, such as, milestone, task, summary, level-of-effort, and dummy.

Actual Cost (AC). Total costs actually incurred and recorded in accomplishing work performed during a given time period for a schedule activity or work breakdown structure component. Actual cost can sometimes be direct labor hours alone, direct costs alone, or all costs including indirect costs. Also known as the actual cost of work performed (ACWP). See also *earned value technique* (EVT).

Actual Cost of Work Performed (ACWP). See *actual cost* (AC).

Actual Duration. The time in calendar units between the actual start date of the schedule activity and either the data date of the project schedule if the schedule activity is in progress or the actual finish date if the schedule activity is complete. See also *activity actual duration* and *project actual duration.*

Actual Finish Date. The point in time that work actually ended on a schedule activity. (Note: In some application areas, the schedule activity is considered "finished" when work is "substantially complete.") See also *activity actual finish date* and *project actual finish date.*

Actual Start Date. See *activity actual start date* and *project actual start date.*

Actual Finish Date (AF). The point in time that work actually ended on a schedule activity. (Note: In some application areas, the schedule activity is considered "finished" when work is "substantially complete.")

Actual Start Date (AS). The point in time that work actually started on a schedule activity.

Application Area. A category of projects that have common components significant in such projects, but are not needed or present in all projects. Application areas are usually defined in terms of either the product (i.e., by similar technologies or production methods) or the type of customer (i.e., internal versus external, government versus commercial) or industry sector (i.e., utilities, automotive, aerospace, information technologies). Application areas can overlap.

Approve. The act of formally confirming, sanctioning, ratifying, or agreeing to something.

Arrow. The graphic presentation of a schedule activity in the arrow diagramming method or a logical relationship between schedule activities in the precedence diagramming method.

Arrow Diagramming Method (ADM) [Technique]. A schedule network diagramming technique in which schedule activities are represented by arrows. The tail of the arrow represents the start, and the head represents the finish of the schedule activity. (The length of the arrow does *not* represent the expected duration of the schedule activity.) Schedule activities are connected at points called nodes (usually drawn as small circles) to illustrate the sequence in which the schedule activities are expected to be performed. See also *precedence diagramming method* (PDM).

As-of Date. See *data date* (DD).

Assumptions [Output/Input]. Assumptions are factors that, for planning purposes, are considered to be true, real, or certain without proof or demonstration. Assumptions affect all aspects of project planning, and are part of the progressive elaboration of the project. Project teams frequently identify, document, and validate assumptions as part of their planning process. Assumptions generally involve a degree of risk.

Author. The originator, publisher, or responsible party of a document, such as a schedule, estimate, or analysis.

Backward Pass. The calculation of late finish dates and late start dates for the uncompleted portions of all schedule activities. Determined by working backwards through the schedule network logic from the project's end date. The end date may be calculated in a forward pass or set by the customer or sponsor. See also *schedule network analysis.*

Bar. A rectangular shaped graphical display object used to represent the occurrence of a data component in a document, such as, a schedule activity in a bar chart whose length is determined by the activity start and end dates corresponding to the timescale used for the bar chart. Bars can overlap or be displayed side by side to indicate progress or baselines.

Bar Chart [Tool]. A graphic display of schedule-related information. In the typical bar chart, schedule activities or work breakdown structure components are listed down the left side of the chart, dates are shown across the top, and activity durations are shown as date-placed horizontal bars. Also known as Gantt chart.

Baseline. The approved time phased plan (for a project, a work breakdown structure component, a work package, or a schedule activity), plus or minus approved project scope, cost, schedule, and technical changes. Generally refers to the current baseline, but may refer to the original or some other baseline. Usually used with a modifier (e.g., cost baseline, schedule baseline, performance measurement baseline, technical baseline). See also *performance measurement baseline.*

Baseline Date. The date on which the current baseline was established. Sometimes used with a modifier such as, project schedule, project scope, or project cost.

Baseline Duration. See *activity baseline duration* and *project baseline duration*.

Baseline Finish Date. See *activity baseline finish date* and *project baseline finish date*.

Baseline Start Date. See *activity baseline start date* and *project baseline start date*.

Budget. The approved estimate for the project or any work breakdown structure component or any schedule activity. See also *estimate*.

Budgeted Cost of Work Performed (BCWP). See *earned value* (EV).

Calendar. A table or register of dates containing the days of each month and week in one or more years. In project management, each date may be identified as a time span for performing work (work period) or as a time span for not performing work including designated holidays (non-work period) and each date may be further subdivided into segments such as shifts, hours, or even minutes that may be designated as work periods or non-work periods. Usually used with a modifier such as, activity, fiscal year, Gregorian, project, program, or resource.

Calendar Library. A set of calendars that can be applied to the various schedule activities and resources. See also *activity calendar* and *resource calendar.*

Calendar Unit. The smallest unit of time used in scheduling the project. Calendar units are generally in hours, days, or weeks, but can also be in quarter years, months, shifts, or even in minutes.

Change Control. Identifying, documenting, approving or rejecting, and controlling changes to the project baseline.

Component. A constituent part, element, or piece of a complex whole.

Constraint [Input]. The state, quality, or sense of being restricted to a given course of action or inaction. An applicable restriction or limitation, either internal or external to the project, that will affect the performance of the project or a process. For example, a schedule constraint is any limitation or restraint placed on the project schedule that affects when a schedule activity can be scheduled and is usually in the form of fixed imposed dates. A cost constraint is any limitation or restraint placed on the project budget such as funds available over time. A project resource constraint is any limitation or restraint placed on resource usage, such as what resource skills or disciplines are available and the amount of a given resource available during a specified time frame.

Control [Technique]. Comparing actual performance with planned performance, analyzing variances, assessing trends to effect process improvements, evaluating possible alternatives, and recommending appropriate corrective action as needed.

Control Account (CA) [Tool]. A management control point where scope, budget (resource plans), actual cost, and schedule are integrated and compared to earned value for performance measurement. Control accounts are placed at selected management points (specific components at selected levels) of the work breakdown structure. Each control account may include one or more work packages, but each work package may be associated with only one control account. Each control account is associated with a specific single organizational component in the organizational breakdown structure (OBS). Previously called a cost account. See also *work package.*

Control Schedule [Process]. The process of controlling changes to the project schedule.

Corrective Action. Documented direction for executing the project work to bring expected future performance of the project work in line with the project management plan.

Cost. The monetary value or price of a project activity or component that includes the monetary worth of the resources required to perform and complete the activity or component, or to produce the component. A specific cost can be composed of a combination of cost components including direct labor hours, other direct costs, indirect labor hours, other indirect costs, and purchased price. (However, in the earned value management methodology, in some instances, the term cost can represent only labor hours without conversion to monetary worth.) See also *actual cost* (AC), *estimate.*

Cost Type. A subdivision of the cost such as, direct cost, indirect cost, and fee.

Cost Component. A component of the cost such as, labor cost, equipment cost, and material cost.

Crashing [Technique]. A specific type of project schedule compression technique performed by taking action to decrease the total project schedule duration after analyzing a number of alternatives to determine how to get the maximum schedule duration compression for the least additional cost. Typical approaches for crashing a schedule include reducing schedule activity durations and increasing the assignment of resources on schedule activities. See also *fast tracking, schedule compression*

Criteria. Standards, rules, or tests on which a judgment or decision can be based, or by which a product, service, result, or process can be evaluated.

Critical Activity. Any schedule activity on a critical path in a project schedule. Most commonly determined by using the critical path method. Although some activities are "critical," in the dictionary sense, without being on the critical path, this meaning is seldom used in the project context.

Critical Chain Method [Technique]. A schedule network analysis technique that modifies the project schedule to account for limited resources. The critical chain method mixes deterministic and probabilistic approaches to schedule network analysis.

Critical Path. Generally, but not always, the sequence of schedule activities determining the duration of the project. Generally, it is the longest path through the project. However, a critical path can end, as an example, on a schedule milestone that is in the middle of the schedule model and that has a finish-no-later-than imposed date schedule constraint. See also *project critical path, specified critical path,* and *critical path method.*

Critical Path Method (CPM) [Technique]. A schedule network analysis technique used to determine the amount of scheduling flexibility (the amount of float) on various logical network paths in the project schedule network, and to determine the minimum total project duration. Early start and finish dates are calculated by means of a forward pass, using a specified start date. Late start and finish dates are calculated by means of a backward pass, starting from a specified completion date, which sometimes is the project early finish date determined during the forward pass calculation. See also *critical path.*

Current Finish Date. The current estimate of the point in time when a schedule activity will be completed, where the estimate reflects any reported work progress. See also *scheduled finish date, activity current finish date,* and *project current finish date.*

Current Start Date. The current estimate of the point in time when a schedule activity will begin, where the estimate reflects any reported work progress. See also *scheduled start date, baseline start date, activity current start date,* and *project current start date.*

Customer. The person or organization that will use the project's product or service or result. See also *user.*

Data Date (DD). The date through which the project status and progress were last determined and reported for analyses, such as scheduling and performance measurements. It is the last past historical date. Also known as as-of-date.

Data Date Line. Vertical line from top to bottom of a graphical report such as a bar chart showing the data date in relationship to the timescale and bars.

Date. A term representing the day, month, and year of a calendar, and, in some instances, the time of day.

Decompose. See *decomposition.*

Decomposition [Technique]. A planning technique that subdivides the project scope and project deliverables into smaller, more manageable components, until the project work, associated with accomplishing the project scope and providing the deliverables, is defined in sufficient detail to support executing, monitoring, and controlling the work.

Deliverable [Output/Input]. Any unique and verifiable product, result, or capability to perform a service that must be produced to complete a process, phase, or project. Often used more narrowly in reference to an external deliverable, which is a deliverable that is subject to approval by the project sponsor or customer. See also *product, result, service.*

Dependency. See *logical relationship.*

Develop Schedule [Process]. The process of analyzing schedule activity sequences, schedule activity durations, resource requirements, and schedule constraints to create the project schedule.

Discipline. A field of work requiring specific knowledge and that has a set of rules governing work conduct (e.g., mechanical engineering, computer programming, cost estimating, etc.).

Document. A medium and the information recorded thereon, that generally has permanence and can be read by a person or a machine. Examples include project management plans, specifications, procedures, studies, and manuals.

Driving Resources. Resources that are considered to have a direct impact on activity duration during resource leveling.

Duration (DU or DUR). The total number of work periods (not including holidays or other nonworking periods) required to complete a schedule activity or work breakdown structure component or project. Usually expressed as work-hours, workdays or workweeks. Sometimes incorrectly equated with elapsed time. Contrast with *effort*. See also *activity duration* and *project duration.*

Duration Percent Complete. See also *activity duration percent complete* and *project duration percent complete.*

Duration Variance. See *activity duration variance* and *project duration variance.*

Early Finish Date (EF). In the critical path method, the earliest possible point in time on which the uncompleted portions of a schedule activity (or the project) can finish, based on the schedule network logic, the data date, and any schedule constraints. Early finish dates can change as the project progresses and as changes are made to the project management plan. See also *activity early finish date* and *project early finish date.*

Early Start Date (ES). In the critical path method, the earliest possible point in time on which the uncompleted portions of a schedule activity (or the project) can start, based on the schedule network logic, the data date, and any schedule constraints. Early start dates can change as the project progresses and as changes are made to the project management plan. See also *activity early start date* and *project early start date.*

Earned Value (EV). The value of work performed expressed in terms of the approved budget assigned to that work for a schedule activity or work breakdown structure component. Also known as budgeted cost of work performed (BCWP).

Earned Value Technique (EVT) [Technique]. A specific technique for measuring the performance of work for a work breakdown structure component, control account, or project. Also referred to as the earning rules and crediting method. See also *actual cost, estimate at completion* (EAC), and *estimate to completion* (EVC).

Effort. The number of labor units required to complete a schedule activity or work breakdown structure component. Usually expressed as staff hours, staff days, or staff weeks. Contrast with *duration.*

Enterprise. A company, business, firm, partnership, corporation, or governmental agency.

Estimate [Output/Input]. A quantitative assessment of the likely amount or outcome. Usually applied to project costs, resources, effort, and durations and is usually preceded by a modifier (i.e., preliminary, conceptual, feasibility, order-of-magnitude, definitive). It should always include some indication of accuracy (e.g., $\pm x$ percent).

Estimate at Completion (EAC) [Output/Input]. The expected total cost of a schedule activity, a work breakdown structure component, or the project when the defined scope of work will be completed. EAC is equal to the actual cost (AC) plus the estimate to complete (ETC) for all of the remaining work. EAC = AC plus ETC. The EAC may be calculated based on performance to date or estimated by the project team based on other factors, in which case it is often referred to as the latest revised estimate. See also *earned value technique* (EVT), *estimate to complete* (ETC).

Estimate to Complete (ETC) [Output/Input]. The expected cost needed to complete all the remaining work for a schedule activity, work breakdown structure component, or the project. See also *earned value technique* (EVT), *estimate at completion* (EAC).

Fast Tracking [Technique]. A specific project schedule compression technique that changes network logic to overlap phases that would normally be done in sequence, such as the design phase and construction phase, or to perform schedule activities in parallel. See also *crashing*, *schedule compression*

Finish Date. A point in time associated with a schedule activity's completion. Usually qualified by one of the following: actual, baseline, current, early, estimated, late, planned, scheduled, or target. See also *activity finish date* and *project finish date.*

Finish Not Earlier Than. A schedule constraint placed on the schedule activity that affects when a schedule activity can be scheduled and is usually in the form of a fixed imposed date. A Finish Not Earlier Than constraint prevents the activity from being scheduled to finish earlier than the imposed date. "Not earlier than" constraints impact only the CPM forward pass calculation and hence only the CPM early dates of a schedule activity.

Finish Not Later Than. A schedule constraint placed on the schedule activity that affects when a schedule activity can be scheduled and is usually in the form of a fixed imposed date. A Finish Not Later Than constraint prevents the activity from being scheduled to finish later than the imposed date. "Not later than" constraints impact only the CPM backward pass calculation and hence the CPM late dates of a schedule activity.

Finish On. A date constraint placed on the schedule activity that requires the schedule activity to finish on a specific date. A Finish On constraint prevents the activity from being scheduled to finish earlier as well as later than the imposed date. Finish On constraints are a combination of a Not Earlier Than and Not Later Than constraints. These impact both the CPM forward and the backward pass calculation and hence both early and late dates. This causes the schedule activity to have a zero total float while its predecessors and successors may have different total float values.

Finish-to-Finish (FF). The logical relationship where completion of work of the successor activity cannot finish until the completion of work of the predecessor activity.

Finish-to-Start (FS). The logical relationship where initiation of work of the successor activity depends upon the completion of work of the predecessor activity.

Float. Also called slack. See also *free float* (FF), *total float* (TF).

Forecasts. Estimates or predictions of conditions and events in the project's future based on information and knowledge available at the time of the forecast. Forecasts are updated and reissued based on work performance information provided as the project is executed. The information is based on the project's past performance and expected future performance, and includes information that could impact the project in the future, such as estimate at completion and estimate to complete.

Forward Pass. The calculation of the early start and early finish dates for the uncompleted portions of all network activities. See also *backward pass*, *schedule network analysis.*

Free Float (FF). The amount of time that a schedule activity can be delayed without delaying the CPM early start of immediately following schedule activities. See also *total float* (TF).

Gantt Chart. See *bar chart*.

Graph. A visual graphical display using lines and shapes to represent data values, such as project status or forecast information.

Hammock Activity. An activity whose duration is aggregated by logical relationships from a group of related activities within the schedule model. See also *summary activity*.

Imposed Date. A fixed date imposed on a schedule activity or schedule milestone, usually in the form of a Start Not Earlier Than and Finish Not Later Than date.

Input [Process Input]. Any item, whether internal or external to the project that is required by a process before that process proceeds. May be an output from a predecessor process.

Integrated. Interrelated, interconnected, interlocked, or meshed components blended and unified into a functioning or unified whole.

Lag [Technique]. A modification of a logical relationship that directs a delay in the successor activity. For example, in a finish-to-start dependency with a ten-day lag, the successor activity cannot start until ten days after the predecessor activity has finished. See also *lead*.

Late Finish Date (LF). In the critical path method, the latest possible point in time that a schedule activity may be completed based upon the schedule network logic, the project completion date, and any constraints assigned to the schedule activities without violating a schedule constraint or delaying the project completion date. The late finish dates are determined during the backward pass calculation of the project schedule network. See also *activity late finish date, project late finish date*.

Late Start Date (LS). In the critical path method, the latest possible point in time that a schedule activity may begin based upon the schedule network logic, the project completion date, and any constraints assigned to the schedule activities without violating a schedule constraint or delaying the project completion date. The late start dates are determined during the backward pass calculation of the project schedule network. See also *activity late start date, project late start date*.

Lead [Technique]. A modification of a logical relationship that allows an acceleration of the successor activity. For example, in a finish-to-start dependency with a ten-day lead, the successor activity can start ten days before the predecessor activity has finished. A negative lead is equivalent to a positive lag. See also *lag*.

Lessons Learned [Output/Input]. The learning gained from the process of performing the project. Lessons learned may be identified at any point. Also considered a project record, to be included in the lessons learned knowledge base.

Level of Effort (LOE). Support-type activity (e.g., seller or customer liaison, project cost accounting, project management, etc.), which does not produce definitive end products. It is generally characterized by a uniform rate of work performance over a period of time determined by the activities supported.

Leveling. See *resource leveling.*

Logic. See *network logic.*

Logic Diagram. See *project schedule network diagram.*

Logical Relationship. A dependency between two project schedule activities, or between a project schedule activity and a schedule milestone. The four possible types of logical relationships are: finish-to-start; finish-to-finish; start-to-start; and start-to-finish. See also *precedence relationship, finish-to-finish* (FF), *finish-to-start* (FS), *start-to-finish,* and *start-to-start.*

Master Schedule [Tool]. A summary-level project schedule that identifies the major deliverables and work breakdown structure components and key schedule milestones. See also *milestone schedule.*

Medium. The type of material used to store a document. Media consist of hard-copy bound material, hard-copy unbound material, soft-copy material, electronic material, firmware, and software.

Methodology. A system of practices, techniques, procedures, and rules used by those who work in a discipline.

Milestone. A significant point or event in the project. See also *schedule milestone.*

Milestone Schedule [Tool]. A summary-level schedule that identifies the major schedule milestones. See also *master schedule.*

Most Likely Duration. The total number of work periods in calendar units assigned to perform the schedule activity, considering all of the variables that could affect performance, and is determined to be the most probable activity duration.

Near-Critical Activity. A schedule activity that has low total float. The concept of near-critical is equally applicable to a schedule activity or schedule network path. The limit below which total float is considered near critical is subject to expert judgment and varies from project to project.

Network. See also *project schedule network diagram.*

Network Analysis. See *schedule network analysis.*

Network Logic. The collection of schedule activity dependencies that makes up a project schedule network diagram.

Network Path. Any continuous series of schedule activities connected with logical relationships in a project schedule network diagram.

Node. One of the defining points of a schedule network; a junction point joined to some or all of the other dependency lines. See also *arrow diagramming method* (ADM) and *precedence diagramming method* (PDM).

Non-work Period. A date or part of a date identified as a time for not performing work including designated holidays. Each date may be further divided into calendar units, such as shifts, hours, or even minutes that may be designated as the specific non-work period.

Open End. An activity with no predecessor, successor, or both. There should be only two activities/milestones in a schedule with open ends: project start and project completion.

Optimistic Duration. The total number of work periods in calendar units assigned to perform the schedule activity, considering all of the variables that could affect performance, and is determined to be the shortest possible duration.

Organization. A group of persons organized for some purpose or to perform some type of work within an enterprise.

Original Duration. The activity duration originally assigned to a schedule activity and not updated as progress is reported on the activity. Typically used for comparison with actual duration and remaining duration when reporting schedule progress. See also *activity original duration, project original duration.*

Output [Process Output]. A product, result, or service generated by a process. May be an input to a successor process.

Percent Complete (PC or PCT). An estimate, expressed as a percent, of the amount of work that has been completed on an activity or a work breakdown structure component.

Perform Integrated Change Control [Process]. The process of reviewing all change requests, approving changes, and controlling changes to deliverables and organizational process assets.

Performance Measurement Baseline. An approved integrated scope-schedule-cost plan for the project work against which project execution is compared to measure and manage performance. Technical and quality parameters may also be included. See also *baseline.*

Pessimistic Duration. The total number of work periods in calendar units assigned to perform the schedule activity, considering all of the variables that could affect performance, and is determined to be the longest possible activity duration.

Phase. See also *project phase.*

Physical Work Progress. The amount of work physically completed on the project or task. This may be different from the amount of effort or money expended on the project or task. Predetermined techniques of claiming physical work progress that were selected during project planning are used to credit earned value when work is partially complete at the time of progress reporting.

Planned Duration. See also *activity original duration* and *project original duration.*

Planned Finish Date (PF). See also *scheduled finish date.*

Planned Start Date (PS). See *scheduled start date.*

Practice. A specific type of professional or management activity that contributes to the execution of a process and that may employ one or more techniques and tools.

Precedence Diagramming Method (PDM) [Technique]. A schedule network diagramming technique in which schedule activities are represented by boxes (or nodes). Schedule activities are graphically linked by one or more logical relationships to show the sequence in which the activities are to be performed. See also *arrow diagramming method* (ADM).

Precedence Relationship. The term used in the precedence diagramming method for a logical relationship. In current usage, however, precedence relationship, logical relationship, and dependency are widely used interchangeably, regardless of the diagramming method used. See also *logical relationship.*

Predecessor Activity. The schedule activity that determines when the logical successor activity can begin or end.

Presentation. An output of a schedule model instance that presents the time based information required by the communication plan, including activities with planned dates, durations, milestone dates, and resource allocation.

Procedure. A series of steps followed in a regular definitive order to accomplish something.

Process. A set of interrelated actions and activities performed to achieve a specified set of products, results, or services.

Product. An artifact that is produced, is quantifiable, and can be either an end item in itself or a component item. Additional words for products are materiel and goods. Contrast with *result* and *service*. See also *deliverable.*

Product Scope. The features and functions that characterize a product, service or result. See also *scope.*

Product Scope Description. The documented narrative description of the product scope.

Progressive Elaboration [Technique]. Continuously improving and detailing a plan as more detailed and specific information and more accurate estimates become available as the project progresses, and thereby producing more accurate and complete plans that result from the successive iterations of the planning process.

Project. A temporary endeavor undertaken to create a unique product, service, or result.

Project Actual Duration. The total number of work periods in calendar units between the project actual start date of the project and either the data date of the schedule model instance, if the project is in progress or the project actual finish date, if the project is complete. See also *actual duration.*

Project Actual Finish Date. The point in time associated with the activity actual finish date of the last schedule activity in the project. See also *actual finish date.*

Project Actual Start Date. The point in time associated with the activity actual start date of the first schedule activity in the project.

Project Attributes. Multiple attributes associated with each unique project that can be included within the schedule model. Project attributes include, but may not be limited to project identifier, project name, project description, project scope statement, project calendar, and assigned resource calendars.

Project Baseline Duration. The total number of work periods in calendar units needed to execute the approved project schedule baseline for the project.

Project Baseline Finish Date. The point in time associated with the completion of the last schedule activity in an approved project schedule baseline. See also *project current finish date*.

Project Baseline Start Date. The point in time associated with the beginning of the first schedule activity in an approved project schedule baseline. See also *project current start date.*

Project Begin Date. The point in time set by the project early start date as determined by a schedule network analysis or as established by a project start constraint. Also known as project start date.

Project Calendar. A calendar of working days or shifts that establishes those dates on which schedule activities are worked and nonworking days that determine those dates on which schedule activities are idle. Typically defines holidays, weekends, and shift hours. See also *resource calendar* and *activity calendar.*

Project Completion Date. See *project end date.*

Project Cost Estimate. The estimated cost for the entire project.

Project Critical Path. The longest schedule network path from the project start date or the current project data date to the project finish date. See also *critical path.*

Project Current Finish Date. The current estimate of the point in time when the last schedule activity in the project will be completed, where the estimate reflects any reported work progress. See also *current finish date, project scheduled finish date*, and *project baseline finish date.*

Project Current Start Date. The current estimate of the point in time when the first schedule activity in the project will begin, where the estimate reflects any reported work progress. See also *current start date, project scheduled start date,* and *project baseline start date.*

Project Description. Documented narrative summary of the *project scope statement.*

Project Duration. The total number of work periods in calendar units between the project early start date and the project early finish date. See also *duration* (DU or DUR).

Project Duration Percent Complete. An estimate, expressed as the percentage that the project actual duration is of the project total duration for a project that has work in progress.

Project Duration Variance. A quantifiable deviation, departure, or divergence away from a given duration for a project.

Project Early Finish Date. The earliest possible point in time associated with the completion of the last schedule activity of the project. See also *early finish date.*

Project Early Start Date. The earliest possible point in time associated with the beginning of the first schedule activity of the project. See also *early start date.*

Project End Date. The point in time set by the project late finish date as determined by a schedule network analysis or as established by a project finish constraint. Also known as project completion date.

Project Finish Constraint. A limitation or restraint placed on the project late finish date that affects when the project must finish and is usually in the form of a fixed imposed date.

Project Finish Date. A point in time associated with the completion of the last schedule activity in a project. Usually qualified by one of the following: actual, baseline, current, early, late, scheduled, or target. See also *finish date.*

Project Finish Variance. A quantifiable deviation, departure, or divergence from a known schedule baseline finish date or project end date. May be expressed as either a percentage or number of work periods.

Project Identifier. A short unique numeric or text identification assigned to each project to differentiate a particular project from other projects in a program.

Project Late Finish Date. The latest possible point in time associated with the completion of the last schedule activity of the project.

Project Late Start Date. The latest possible point in time associated with the beginning of the first schedule activity of the project.

Project Management Plan [Output/Input]. A formal, approved document that defines how the project is executed, monitored, and controlled. It may be summary or detailed and may be composed of one or more subsidiary management plans and other planning documents.

Project Management Software [Tool]. A class of computer software applications specifically designed to aid the project management team with planning, monitoring, and controlling the project, including: cost estimating, scheduling, communications, collaboration, configuration management, document control, records management, and risk analysis.

Project Management Team. The members of the project team who are directly involved in project management activities. On some smaller projects, the project management team may include virtually all of the project team members.

Project Manager (PM). The person assigned by the performing organization to achieve the project objectives.

Project Name. A short phrase or label for each *project*, used in conjunction with the *project identifier* to differentiate a particular project from other projects in a *program*. Also known as project title.

Project Original Duration. The initial estimate of the total number of work periods in calendar units needed to complete a project. Typically determined from the initial longest network path though the project.

Project Phase. A collection of logically related project activities, usually culminating in the completion of a major deliverable. Project phases (also called phases) are mainly completed sequentially, but can overlap in some project situations. Phases can be subdivided into subphases and then components; this hierarchy, if the project or portions of the project are divided into phases, is contained in the work breakdown structure. A project phase is a component of a project life cycle. A project phase is not a Project Management Process Group.

Project Physical Percent Complete. A calculation, expressed as a percent, of the amount of *work* that has been completed on the project, measured in terms of physical work progress.

Project Planned Finish Date. See also *project scheduled finish date.*

Project Planned Start Date. See also *project scheduled start date.*

Project Remaining Duration. The total number of work periods in calendar units, between the data date of the schedule model and the project early finish date of a project that has at least one activity actual start date. This represents the time needed to complete a project where the work is in progress. See also *remaining duration.*

Project Schedule [Output/Input]. An output of a schedule model instance that presents the time based information required by the communication plan, including activities with planned dates, durations, milestone dates, and resource allocation. See also *presentation.*

Project Schedule Network Diagram [Output/Input]. Any schematic display of the logical relationships among the project schedule activities. Always drawn from left to right to reflect project work chronology.

Project Scheduled Finish Date. The point in time when work was scheduled to complete on a project. The project scheduled finish date is normally within the range of dates delimited by the project early finish date and the project late finish date. It may reflect finish resource leveling of scarce resources. Sometimes called project planned finish date. See also *project current finish date, scheduled finish date.*

Project Scheduled Start Date. The point in time when work was scheduled to begin on the project. The project scheduled start date is normally within the range of dates delimited by the project early start date and the project late start date. It may reflect start resource leveling of scarce resources. Also known as project planned start date. See also *project current start date, scheduled start date.*

Project Scope. The work that must be performed to deliver a product, service, or result with the specified features and functions. See also *scope.*

Project Scope Statement [Output/Input]. The narrative description of the project scope, including major deliverables, project objectives, project assumptions, project constraints, and a statement of work, that provides a documented basis for making future project decisions and for confirming or developing a common understanding of project scope among the stakeholders. The definition of the project scope—what needs to be accomplished.

Project Sponsor. See *sponsor.*

Project Stakeholder. See *stakeholder.*

Project Start Constraint. A limitation or restraint placed on the project early start date that affects when the project must start and is usually in the form of a fixed imposed date.

Project Start Date. A point in time associated with the beginning of the first schedule activity in a project. Usually qualified by one of the following: actual, baseline, current, early, late, scheduled, or target. See also *start date.*

Project Target Date Variance. A quantifiable deviation, departure, or divergence away from a known project target start date or project target finish date.

Project Target Duration. The estimated total number of work periods in calendar units, needed to complete the project as determined by a specific project target schedule.

Project Target Finish Date. The scheduler-selected point in time established by schedule network analysis for completion of a specific version of the project schedule.

Project Target Start Date. The scheduler-selected point in time established by schedule network analysis for beginning a specific version of the project schedule.

Project Team. All the project team members, including the project management team, the project manager and, for some projects, the project sponsor.

Project Team Members. The persons who report either directly or indirectly to the project manager, and who are responsible for performing project work as a regular part of their assigned duties.

Project Time Management [Knowledge Area]. Project Time Management includes the processes required to accomplish timely completion of the project. The Project Time Management processes include Define Activities, Sequence Activities, Estimate Activity Resources, Estimate Activity Durations, Develop Schedule, and Control Schedule.

Project Title. See *project name.*

Project Total Duration. The total number of work periods in calendar units to complete a project. For a project in progress, it includes the project actual duration plus the project remaining duration.

Project Work. See *work.*

Relationship Line. A logical relationship line drawn within a project schedule network diagram from one schedule activity to one or more other schedule activities indicating the type of logical relationship by the relative position of the beginning and end points of the line.

Remaining Duration (RD). The time in calendar units, (a) equal to the original duration for an activity that has not started or (b) between the data date of the project schedule and the finish date of a schedule activity that has an actual start date. This represents the time needed to complete a schedule activity where the work is in progress. See also *activity remaining duration, project remaining duration.*

Report Column. A vertical display area in the document body representing one data component or piece of information, such as a project group, activity group, or resource group.

Report Data Description. A short text description of a data component in the report.

Report Gridlines. Horizontal and vertical lines within a document corresponding to data components, such as timescale units or rows in a bar chart.

Report Row. A horizontal display area in the document body representing one data component or piece of information, such as an activity group or resource group.

Report Table. A display formatted in report rows and report columns, such as a document that presents time-scaled columnar schedule-related information.

Requirement. A condition or capability that must be met or possessed by a system, product, service, result, or component to satisfy a contract, standard, specification, or other formally imposed documents. Requirements include the quantified and documented needs, wants, and expectations of the sponsor, customer, and other stakeholders.

Resource. Skilled human resources (specific disciplines either individually or in crews or teams), equipment, services, supplies, commodities, budgets, or funds.

Resource Application. The percent of the resource duration that the assigned resource is estimated to apply to the work of the schedule activity.

Resource Assignment. The linkage of one or more resources to a schedule activity and identification of the amount of each resource that is needed to accomplish the work on that schedule activity.

Resource Attributes. Multiple attributes associated with each resource that can be included within the resource library. Resource attributes include resource identifier, resource name, resource type, resource availability, resource rate, resource code, constraints, and assumptions.

Resource Availability. The dates and number of work periods in calendar units that a given resource is available according to the appropriate resource calendar.

Resource Calendar. A calendar of working days and nonworking days that determines those *dates* on which each specific resource is idle or can be active. Typically defines resource specific holidays and resource availability periods. See also *calendar library, project calendar* and *activity calendar.*

Resource-Constrained Schedule. See *resource-limited schedule.*

Resource Dictionary. See *resource library.*

Resource Duration. The number of work periods in calendar units the assigned resource is estimated to spend on executing the work of the schedule activity.

Resource Group. A project team member selected set of resources sharing some common resource attribute that allows those resources to be reported or displayed separately such as being grouped in a graphic display.

Resource Identifier. A short unique numeric or text identification assigned to each specific resource to differentiate that resource from other resources. Resource identifiers are typically unique within any one project.

Resource Lag. The number of calendar units a resource is to wait after the activity start date before beginning work on the schedule activity.

Resource Leveling [Technique]. Any form of schedule network analysis in which scheduling decisions (start and finish dates) are driven by resource constraints (e.g., limited resource availability or difficult-to-manage changes in resource availability levels). See also *resource-limited schedule* and *schedule network analysis.*

Resource Library. A documented tabulation containing the complete list, including resource attributes, of all resources that can be assigned to project activities. Also known as resource dictionary.

Resource-Limited Schedule. A project schedule whose schedule activity, scheduled start dates and scheduled finish dates reflect expected resource availability. A resource-limited schedule does not have any early or late start or finish dates. The resource-limited schedule total float is determined by calculating the difference between the critical path method late finish date and the resource-limited scheduled finish date. Also known as resource-constrained schedule. See also *resource leveling.*

Resource Name. A short phrase or label for each resource used in conjunction with a resource identifier to differentiate that resource from other resources. The resource name normally differentiates a resource by type, role, or individual.

Resource Planning. See *activity resource estimating.*

Resource Rate. The unit cost rate assigned to a specific resource, including known rate escalations.

Resource Type. A unique designation that differentiates a resource by skills, capabilities or other attributes.

Result. An output from performing project management processes and activities. Results include outcomes (e.g., integrated systems, revised process, restructured organization, tests, trained personnel, etc.) and documents (e.g., policies, plans, studies, procedures, specifications, reports, etc.). Contrast with product and service. See also *deliverable.*

Role. A defined function to be performed by a project team member, such as testing, filing, inspecting, coding.

Schedule. See *project schedule* and *schedule model.*

Schedule Activity. A discrete scheduled component of work performed during the course of a project. A schedule activity normally has an estimated duration, an estimated cost, and estimated resource requirements. Schedule activities are connected to other schedule activities or schedule milestones with logical relationships, and are decomposed from work packages. See also *activity.*

Schedule Analysis. See also *schedule network analysis.*

Schedule Compression [Technique]. Shortening the project schedule duration without reducing the project scope. See also *crashing* and *fast tracking.*

Schedule Compression. Techniques used to shorten the schedule duration without reducing the project scope.

Schedule Level. A project team specified rule for the relative granularity of schedule activities in the overall schedule model.

Schedule Milestone. A significant event in the project schedule, such as an event restraining future work or marking the completion of a major deliverable. A schedule milestone has zero duration. Also known as milestone activity. See also *milestone.*

Schedule Model [Tool]. A dynamic representation of the plan for executing the project's activities developed by the project stakeholders applying the scheduling method to a scheduling tool using project specific data such as activity lists and activity attributes. The schedule model can be processed by a scheduling tool to produce various schedule model instances. (scheduling method plus scheduling tool plus project specific data equal schedule model).

Schedule Model Instance [Tool]. A copy of the schedule model, that has been processed by a schedule tool and has reacted to inputs and adjustments made to the project specific data within the scheduling tool (completed update cycle), that is saved for record and reference, such as data date version, target schedule models and the baseline schedule model. The instances produce various schedule presentations such as critical paths, resource profiles, activity assignments, record of accomplishments, etc. and can provide time-based forecasts, throughout the project's life cycle. When used together, the instances support analysis, such as variance analysis.

Schedule Network Analysis [Technique]. The technique of identifying early and late start dates, as well as early and late finish dates, for the uncompleted portions of project schedule activities. See also *backward pass, critical path method, critical chain method,* and *resource leveling.*

Schedule Performance Index (SPI). A measure of schedule efficiency on a project. It is the ratio of earned value (EV) to planned value (PV). The SPI = EV divided by PV. An SPI equal to or greater than one indicates a favorable condition and a value of less than one indicates an unfavorable condition. See also *earned value technique* (EVT).

Schedule Variance (SV). A measure of schedule performance on a project. It is the algebraic difference between the earned value (EV) and the planned value (PV). SV = EV minus PV. See also *earned value technique* (EVT).

Scheduled Finish Date (SF). The point in time that work was scheduled to finish on a schedule activity. The scheduled finish date is normally within the range of dates delimited by the early finish date and the late finish date. It may reflect resource leveling of scarce resources. Sometimes called planned finish date. See *also current finish date, activity scheduled finish date, project scheduled finish date.*

Scheduled Start Date (SS). The point in time that work was scheduled to start on a schedule activity. The scheduled start date is normally within the range of dates delimited by the early start date and the late start date. It may reflect resource leveling of scarce resources. Sometimes called planned start date. See also *current start date, activity scheduled start date, project scheduled start date.*

Scheduling Method. A system of practices, techniques, procedures and rules used by project scheduling schedulers. This methodology can be performed either manually or with project management software specifically used for scheduling.

Scheduling Tool [Tool]. A tool which provides schedule component names, definitions, structural relationships, and formats that support the application of a scheduling method.

Scope. The sum of the products, services, and results to be provided as a project. See also *project scope* and *product scope.*

Service. Useful work performed that does not produce a tangible product or result, such as performing any of the business functions supporting production or distribution. Contrast with *product* and *result.* See also *deliverable.*

Slack. See *total float* (TF) and *free float* (FF).

Specification. A document that specifies, in a complete, precise, verifiable manner, the requirements, design, behavior, or other characteristics of a system, component, product, result, or service and, often, the procedures for determining whether these provisions have been satisfied. Examples are: requirement specification, design specification, product specification, and test specification.

Specified Critical Path. The longest sequence of schedule activities in a project team member specified schedule network path. See also *critical path.*

Sponsor. The person or group that provides the financial resources, in cash or in kind, for the project.

Stakeholder. Person or organization (e.g., customer, sponsor, performing organization, or the public) that is actively involved in the project, or whose interests may be positively or negatively affected by execution or completion of the project. A stakeholder may also exert influence over the project and its deliverables.

Standard. A document established by consensus and approved by a recognized body that provides, for common and repeated use, rules, guidelines or characteristics for activities or their results, aimed at the achievement of the optimum degree of order in a given context.

Start Date. A point in time associated with a schedule activity's start, usually qualified by one of the following: actual, planned, estimated, scheduled, early, late, target, baseline, or current. See also *activity start date, project start date.*

Start Not Earlier Than. A schedule constraint placed on the schedule activity that affects when a schedule activity can be scheduled and is usually in the form of a fixed imposed date. A Start Not Earlier Than constraint prevents the schedule activity from being scheduled to start earlier than the imposed date.

Start Not Later Than. A schedule constraint placed on the schedule activity that affects when a schedule activity can be scheduled and is usually in the form of a fixed imposed date. A Start Not Later Than constraint prevents the schedule activity from being scheduled to start later than the imposed date.

Start On. A schedule constraint placed on the schedule activity that affects when a schedule activity can be scheduled and is usually in the form of a fixed imposed date. A Start On constraint requires the schedule activity to start on a specific date.

Start-to-Finish (SF). The logical relationship where completion of the successor schedule activity is dependent upon the initiation of the predecessor schedule activity. See also *logical relationship.*

Start-to-Start (SS). The logical relationship where initiation of the work of the successor schedule activity depends upon the initiation of the work of the predecessor schedule activity. See also *logical relationship.*

Statement of Work (SOW). A narrative description of products, services, or results to be supplied.

Status Date. A term whose meaning for status data reporting varies by the brand of project management software used for scheduling, where in some systems the status date is included in the past and in some systems the status date is in the future. See also *data date* or *time-now date.*

Subnetwork. A subdivision (fragment) of a project schedule network diagram, usually representing a subproject or a work package. Often used to illustrate or study some potential or proposed schedule condition, such as changes in preferential schedule logic or project scope. See also *summary activity.*

Subphase. A subdivision of a phase.

Subproject. A smaller portion of the overall project created when a project is subdivided into more manageable components or pieces. Subprojects are usually represented in the work breakdown structure. A subproject can be referred to as a project, managed as a project, and acquired from a seller. May be referred to as a subnetwork in a project schedule network diagram. See also *summary activity.*

Substantial Completion. The point when the schedule network logic and deliverable requirements of the schedule activity are satisfied and the successor activities can begin.

Successor. See *successor activity.*

Successor Activity. The schedule activity that follows a predecessor activity, as determined by their logical relationship.

Summary Activity. A single representation of activities aggregated by common attributes within the schedule model. See also *subproject* and *subnetwork*.

System. An integrated set of regularly interacting or interdependent components created to accomplish a defined objective, with defined and maintained relationships among its components, and the whole producing or operating better than the simple sum of its components. Systems may be either physically process based or management process based, or more commonly a combination of both. Systems for project management are composed of project management processes, techniques, methodologies, and tools operated by the project management team.

Target Duration. See Activity *target duration* and *project target duration.*

Target Finish Date. See *activity target finish date* and *project target finish date.*

Target Schedule. A schedule adopted for comparison purposes during schedule network analysis, which can be different from the baseline schedule. See also *baseline.*

Target Start Date. See *activity target start date* and *project target start date.*

Task. A term for work whose meaning and placement within a structured plan for project work varies by the application area, industry, and brand of project management software.

Team Members. See *project team members.*

Technique. A defined systematic procedure employed by a human resource to perform an activity to produce a product or result or deliver a service, and that may employ one or more tools.

Template. A partially complete document in a predefined format that provides a defined structure for collecting, organizing and presenting information and data. Templates are often based upon documents created during prior projects. Templates can reduce the effort needed to perform work and increase the consistency of results.

Three-Point Estimate [Technique]. An analytical technique that uses three cost or duration estimates to represent the optimistic, most likely, and pessimistic scenarios. This technique is applied to improve the accuracy of the estimates of cost or duration when the underlying activity or cost component is uncertain.

Time-Now Date. See *data date.*

Timescale. A graduated marking of linear time, which displays time in specific units such as hours, days, weeks, months, quarters, or years. Timescales can show more than one unit of time. Usually shown above or below the data components within a document or electronic graphical display.

Tool. Something tangible, such as a template or software program, used in performing an activity to produce a product or result.

Total Duration. See *activity total duration* and *project total duration.*

Total Float (TF). The total amount of time that a schedule activity may be delayed from its CPM early start date or CPM early finish date without delaying the project end date, or violating a schedule constraint. Calculated using the critical path method technique and determining the difference between the CPM early finish dates and CPM late finish dates. See also (*float, free float* FF).

Unit of Measure. A designation of the type of quantity being measured, such as work-hours, cubic yards, or lines of code.

User. The person or organization that will use the project's product or service. See also *customer.*

Variance. A quantifiable deviation, departure, or divergence away from a known baseline or expected value.

Variance Threshold. A predetermined range of normal outcomes that is determined during the planning process and sets the boundaries within which the team practices management by exception.

Work. Sustained physical or mental effort, exertion, or exercise of skill to overcome obstacles and achieve an objective.

Work Breakdown Structure (WBS) [Output/Input]. A deliverable-oriented hierarchical decomposition of the work to be executed by the project team to accomplish the project objectives and create the required deliverables. It organizes and defines the total scope of the project. Each descending level represents an increasingly detailed definition of the project work. The WBS is decomposed into work packages. The deliverable orientation of the hierarchy includes both internal and external deliverables. See also *work package, control account* (CA), and *contract work breakdown structure* (CWBS).

Work Breakdown Structure Component. An entry in the work breakdown structure that can be at any level.

WBS Element Identifier. A short unique numeric or text identification assigned to each work breakdown structure (WBS) element or component to differentiate a particular WBS element from other WBS elements. The WBS element identifier is typically unique within any complete work breakdown structure.

Work Package. A deliverable or project work component at the lowest level of each branch of the work breakdown structure. The work package includes the schedule activities and schedule milestones required to complete the work package deliverable or project work component. See also *control account* (CA).

Work Performance Information [Output/Input]. Information and data, on the status of the project schedule activities being performed to accomplish the project work, collected as part of the direct and manage project execution processes. Information includes: status of deliverables; implementation status for change requests, corrective actions, preventive actions, and defect repairs; forecasted estimates to complete; reported percent of work physically completed; achieved value of technical performance measures; start and finish dates of schedule activities.

Work Period. A date or part of a date identified as a time for performing work. Each date may be further divided into calendar units, such as shifts, hours, or even minutes that may be designated as the specific work period.

Workaround [Technique]. A response to a negative risk that has occurred. Distinguished from contingency plan in that a workaround is not planned in advance of the occurrence of the risk event.

INDEX